INTERNATIONAL DEVELOPMENT IN PRACTICE

Competency-Based Accounting Education, Training, and Certification

An Implementation Guide

Alfred Borgonovo, Brian Friedrich, and Michael Wells

WORLD BANK GROUP

Contents

Foreword

Relevant information that faithfully represents underlying economic events is undoubtedly fundamental to optimal investment decision-making and capital markets operation, and the consequential link to economic growth and job creation is well known. Therefore, the Governance Global Practice (GGP) of the World Bank has been at the forefront of supporting client countries to develop credible frameworks and capacity for reliable financial reporting. A professional accounting organization (PAO) is a core part of this framework, and PAO strength is necessary to building sustainable financial reporting capacity in a country.

A major task of a full-fledged PAO is to establish a qualification system as well as continuing professional development and education for accountants and auditors in the country. This requires developing a competency framework and defining and/or developing the supporting education and training system. This framework and system must be designed to ensure compliance with the International Accounting Education Standards. In many countries, this requires a serious reform of the accounting education system. The concepts of outcome-based learning, lifelong learning, practical experience requirements and integrative examinations as well as the new skills demanded of professional accountants (ranging from teamwork to critical thinking skills) have turned the reform of accounting education into a complex undertaking. Mature economies do not always offer clear pathways for developing and transitioning economies to follow, given the different educational and professional traditions and certification models of transitioning economies, as well as their challenges in adapting accounting education to the modern economy. The International Education Standards—developed by the International Accounting Education Standards Board™—however, offer a well-defined framework for PAOs to work with. But local stakeholders need to agree on how this framework should be adapted to suit local conditions, taking into account the capacity of local institutions, legal traditions and government policy as well as many other constraints and obstacles.

In view of the above, there is, therefore, a need for some guidance to implement accounting education reforms. The Competency-Based Accounting Education, Training and Certification Implementation Guide developed by the World Bank Centre for Financial Reporting Reform (CFRR) seeks to do just that.

The guide is a useful companion to governments and national stakeholders who are embarking on accounting education reforms as well as development partners or international organizations that are supporting that effort. Practical competence, as opposed to theoretical knowledge, is central to the transformation of the accounting education required for today's economy.

I warmly commend this work to all who are interested and involved in accounting education reforms.

Ed Olowo-Okere
Director, Governance Global Practice
The World Bank

Acknowledgments

Competency-Based Accounting Education, Training, and Certification: An Implementation Guide was developed by a team from the World Bank's Centre for Financial Reporting Reform (CFRR), led by Alfred Borgonovo, Senior Financial Management Specialist, and including consultants Brian Friedrich and Michael Wells. Editorial assistance was provided by Oleksiy Manuilov and Ecaterina Gusarova. Anara Tokusheva, Program Assistant, CFRR, provided administrative support throughout the project. The project was supervised by both Jarett Decker, Head, CFRR, and Adenike Sherifat Oyeyiola, Practice Manager, World Bank.

The team would like to extend special thanks to Laura Friedrich, Principal at friedrich & friedrich corp., and Nancy Foran, Vice President, International, at CPA Canada for their critical support and assistance throughout the project.

The team is grateful for the guidance and feedback provided by the peer reviewers for this project: Moses Wasike, Lead Financial Management Specialist; Patrick Kabuya, Senior Financial Management Specialist; and Zohra Farooq Nooryar, Senior Financial Management Specialist. The team is also grateful to Bonnie Ann Sirois, Senior Financial Management Specialist, and Abbas Hasan Kizilbash, Senior Financial Management Specialist, for their comments and feedback.

The team also wishes to thank Cristian Aedo, Practice Manager, and Dingyong Hou, Senior Education Specialist, both of the World Bank; David McPeak, Principal, International Accounting Education Standards Board; Anna-Marie Christian, Director, International Programs at CPA Canada; Mark Campbell, Head of International Capacity Building at Institute of Chartered Accountants in England and Wales (ICAEW); and David Brookfield, Consultant, ICAEW, whose contributions were invaluable throughout the development of the guide. This publication was completed under the STAREP Program, which is supported by the Austrian Development Agency, the Federal Ministry of Finance of the Republic of Austria, and the European Union's EU 4 Business initiative, and is carried out under the REPARIS Multidonor Trust Fund.

About the Authors

Alfred Borgonovo joined the World Bank's Centre for Financial Reporting Reform (CFRR) as a Senior Financial Management Specialist in 2015. He is a member of both CPA Australia and CPA Canada. Borgonovo worked for CGA Canada for over seven years, in the areas of education and international development, where he played a leading role in shaping international collaboration projects. Prior to this, he worked in various roles ranging from credit analyst to financial controller for several companies including Banque Nationale de Paris, Orange Business Services, NCR Corporation, and the Queensland Department of Education. Over the past 15 years, Alfred has led or participated in many capacity-building projects in the area of accounting education reform in Latin America and the Caribbean, Europe and Central Asia, Southeast Asia, and Africa. Borgonovo is a native French speaker and is fluent in Spanish. He is a PhD candidate in economics at the University of Strathclyde, Glasgow, United Kingdom.

Brian Friedrich has focused on building institutional capacity, implementing competency-based education and experience assessments, and developing strategic, policy, program, governance, and ethics guidance for established and emerging professional and regulatory organizations for over 20 years. Prior to this, he held roles in education and external audit. Friedrich is a member of the International Ethics Standards Board for Accountants and CPA Canada's Public Trust Committee and its Foresight: Future of the Profession working group. He served on the board of CPA British Columbia, and one of its legacy bodies, for 10 years—including as chair. Friedrich also chaired the legacy organization's Ethics and Discipline committees for numerous years. He was awarded a life membership in 2014 for his service to the profession in education, ethics, and governance. Outside of the profession, he has served on a number of boards and committees and is currently a director on the Real Estate Board of Greater Vancouver.

Michael Wells is Professor of Practice at Imperial College Business School and a World Bank consultant, working to deepen understanding of international financial reporting requirements and fostering capacity to make, audit, and regulate the judgments necessary to apply them. For over a decade, he led the International Accounting Standards Board's (IASB) Education Initiative. He serves on the

American Accounting Association (AAA) Membership Advisory Committee. Before that he served on the AAA Education Committee and the AAA Innovation in Accounting Education Award Committee. For nearly a decade he served as a member of the International Federation of Accountants (IFAC) International Accounting Education Standards Board (IAESB) Consultative Advisory Group (CAG) and as a member of the International Association for Accounting Education Research (IAAER) Board of Advisors.

Abbreviations

AAA	American Accounting Association
AACSB	Association to Advance Collegiate Schools of Business International
ABWA	Accountancy Bodies in West Africa
ACCA	Association of Chartered Certified Accountants
AEC	ASEAN Economic Community
AFA	ASEAN Federation of Accountants
AICPA	American Institute of Certified Public Accountants
APC	Assessment of Professional Competence
ATE	authorized training employer
BoA	Board of Accountancy
BOE	Board of Examiners
BS	bachelor of science
BSA	BS in Accountancy
BSAIS	BS in Accounting Information Systems
BSIA	BS in Internal Audit
BSMA	BS in Management Accounting
CA	Chartered Accountant
CAPA	Confederation of Asian and Pacific Accountants
CBAETC	Competency-Based Accounting Education, Training and Certification
CCP	Common Content Project
CFRR	Centre for Financial Reporting Reform
CHED	Commission on Higher Education
CIPFA	Chartered Institute of Public Finance and Accountancy
CPA	Chartered Professional Accountant
CPD	Continuing Professional Development
CTA	Certificate of Theory in Accounting
DE	Diploma Exam
FAQ	frequently asked questions
FASSET	Finance and Accounting Services Sector Education and Training
IAESB™	International Accounting Education Standards Board™

IAS®	IAS® Standards
IASB®	International Accounting Standards Board
ICAEW	Institute of Chartered Accountants in England and Wales
ICAG	Institute of Chartered Accountants of Ghana
ICAS	Institute of Chartered Accountants of Scotland
IESBA®	International Ethics Standards Board for Accountants®
IES™	International Education Standards™
IFAC®	International Federation of Accountants®
IFRS	International Financial Reporting Standards
IPD	Initial Professional Development
ISA®	International Standards on Auditing®
ITC	Initial Test of Competence
MRA	Mutual Recognition Agreements
PACPA	Palestinian Association of Certified Public Accountants
PAEF	Philippine Accountancy Education Framework
PAO	Professional Accountancy Organization
PICPA	Philippine Institute of Certified Public Accountants
PQ	professional qualification
PRC	Professional Regulatory Commission
PWAT	Palestinian Women Accounting Technicians
ROSC A&A	Report on the Observance of Standards and Codes in Accounting and Auditing
SAAA	Serbian Association of Accountants and Auditors
SAICA	South African Institute of Chartered Accountants
SMOs	Statements of Membership Obligations
TBS	task-based simulations

Introduction

WHO IS THIS GUIDE FOR?

This guide is for all those responsible for accounting education, training, or certification. It is particularly relevant to Professional Accountancy Organizations (PAOs) and other bodies that provide or oversee formal education or practical experience that forms part of the initial professional development (IPD) of aspiring professional accountants, or the continuing professional development (CPD) of professional accountants. It is also intended for policy makers and regulators who determine which organizations are licensed to certify professional accountants and related specializations, for example, audit professionals.

Chapter 2 of the Guide is aimed at higher-level decision makers and those overseeing the Competency-Based Accounting Education, Training and Certification (CBAETC) process. This includes individuals with the responsibility for resource-allocation decisions and determining whether CBAETC will be mandated in their jurisdiction. Chapter 3 is intended to more specifically support front-line CBAETC implementers and operational-level decision-makers.

Note that throughout the Guide, guidance is given as to who to include in the various stages of the process. This guidance recognizes that different organizations will approach CBAETC in different ways, based in part on their existing and available resources and current levels of experience with competency-based programs. The Guide does not prescribe specific roles; roles will depend greatly on legislation, resources, and expertise; adding prescriptive expectations would be presumptive.

Although this Guide focuses on professional education, there is some relevance to those developing technician-level accounting programs as well. Accounting technicians benefit from education that focuses on the application of technical knowledge and the development of enabling skills such as critical thinking and analysis.

The guide supports transitioning accounting education, training, and certification from a knowledge-based approach to a competency-based approach. Underlying this shift is the expanding expectation for accountants to demonstrate increased higher-order critical thinking skills and apply professional judgment in response to greater transaction complexity, interconnectedness of entities, and broader global influences.

The purpose of the guide is to:

- Support understanding the gap between the current skills of many accountants in some regions and the skills that are relevant in increasingly digitized and globalized economies
- Convey the essential features of (CBAETC)
- Provide a common reference framework for organizations pursuing CBAETC and the consultants working with them
- Assist countries in developing in-country plans and implementing in-country processes that produce accountants with higher-order skills relevant to their economy's rapidly evolving needs; and, ultimately
- Improve financial reporting, auditing, and regulation.

This guide complements and builds on the requirements established by the International Accounting Education Standards Board™ (IAESB™)'s International Education Standards (IES™).

Implementing CBAETC requires that an organization has reached sufficient maturity to be able to commit the necessary resources for sustainable change. To gain insight into the maturity of the profession, it is useful to consider the level of compliance with the IFAC® Statements of Member Obligations (SMOs). The IFAC document *International Standards: 2017 Global Status Report* presents information regarding the status of compliance with the SMOs among the organizations surveyed. The report provides the following summary information:

Significant progress has been made with adoption of international standards and best practices, reflecting strong support for and commitment to high-quality financial reporting and auditing; greater transparency and accountability; and support for the ethical standards for the accountancy profession. Across the 80 jurisdictions in which 104 member organizations operate:

- 84 percent of jurisdictions (67) have established QA review systems, with 46 percent (37) adopting all SMO 1 requirements for QA reviews of all mandatory audits
- 100 percent of jurisdictions (80) have incorporated some requirements of the 2010 IES, with 20 percent (16) fully adopting all IES for all professional accountants
- 79 percent of jurisdictions (63) have adopted International Standards on Auditing® (ISA®) for all mandatory audits with 70 percent (56) having adopted at least the 2009 Clarified ISA and 9 percent (7) having adopted the new 2016 ISA.2
- 61 percent of jurisdictions (49) have fully adopted the *International Code of Ethics for Professional Accountants™* (the Code™), which refers to the adoption of at least the 2009 Code
- 55 percent of jurisdictions (44) have made strides in the adoption of International Public Sector Accounting Standards® (IPSAS®), with 9 percent (7) fully adopting all IPSAS for all public sector entities.
- 98 percent of jurisdictions (79) have established [Investigation & Discipline] systems, with 15 percent (12) adopting all SMO 6 requirements for all professional accountants

- 91 percent of jurisdictions (72) have adopted IFRS® Standards (IFRS) for all or most public interest entities (International Federation of Accountants 2017).

These results present a positive view of the opportunities available for implementing CBAETC. The profession appears mature enough to be ready to undertake CBAETC, but with only 20 percent of responding organizations having fully implemented the IESs, there are significant gains to be achieved through the pursuit of CBAETC.

Readers representing PAOs should consider their organization's IFAC compliance evaluation in determining which parts of the Guide may be of greatest relevance to them.

WHAT IS PROFESSIONAL COMPETENCE?

Competence is the ability to execute, in the real world, relevant tasks to a specified level of proficiency. Knowledge and understanding alone do not result in competence. Competence requires the effective *application* of relevant skills and particular attributes, which is usually only possible after undertaking specific practical experience.

In an accounting context, **professional competence** is the ability to demonstrate the necessary technical and professional skills, values, ethics, and attitudes at sufficient levels of proficiency to fulfill the role of a professional accountant in a manner that meets the needs and expectations of employers, clients, peers, and the public. Technical knowledge is necessary, but not sufficient, to the accountant's role—professional accountants bring value to society not just by knowing how to account for transactions or determine tax compliance, but more importantly through exercising **professional judgment** by, for example:

- Helping to evaluate risk
- Monitoring and ensuring quality and transparency of financial reporting
- Providing leadership in ethical decision-making
- Evaluating complex transactions and emerging issues to ensure financial reporting remains relevant and useful for users
- Interpreting and applying relevant standards and regulation
- Approaching information with a critical and questioning mindset
- Participating in strategic planning.

It is through the application of professional judgment and competence that professional accountants support business decision-making that fosters public trust, as well as economic stability and growth.

WHAT IS COMPETENCY-BASED ACCOUNTING EDUCATION, TRAINING, AND CERTIFICATION (CBAETC)?

Competency-based education focuses on developing competence rather than just knowledge, which can be best understood by contrasting the two approaches (table 1.1).

Similarly, competency-based training and certification go beyond imparting and requiring knowledge, and focus on developing and requiring demonstration of desired tasks and outcomes at pre-determined levels of proficiency.

TABLE 1.1 **Comparison of competency-based education and knowledge-based education**

KNOWLEDGE-BASED APPROACH	COMPETENCY-BASED APPROACH
Tests "Do you know how to…?"	Tests "Can you…?"
Focuses on what principles, concepts, facts or procedures need to be learned	Focuses on what tasks or outcomes need to be demonstrated
Focuses on theory and concepts	Focuses on practical application of theory
Sets minimum pass marks for percentage of knowledge that needs to be learned and conveyed in assessments	Sets minimum proficiency levels to be attained and demonstrated in order to be deemed sufficiently competent for a role
Often includes rote learning and tests memory	Includes hands-on learning and active engagement, and tests application of knowledge and skills in relevant contexts

Knowledge-based systems are still prevalent in many regions around the world. This approach is severely limited, however, in that it doesn't prepare professionals for the judgment-rich work context that they will face throughout their careers.

Consequently, CBAETC involves equipping aspiring accountants (and up skilling professional accountants) with the professional competencies needed to provide services that are relevant in the globalized and rapidly digitizing age in which business transactions are increasingly complex.

WHY DOES CBAETC MATTER?

PAOs are responsible for ensuring member competence in order to:

- Protect the public
- Protect the reputation of the profession and maintain public trust
- Comply with national standards and regulations
- Meet international requirements and expectations.

CBAETC helps PAOs ensure that professional accountants have the ability to perform their roles to a standard that serves the broad public interest. The roles of professional accountants are varied and have a fundamental impact on decision-making throughout the business world. At the core of the professional accountant's role is the ability to prepare, present, audit, interpret and explain financial and other business information in a manner that protects and serves the public. The faithful representation of financial information is relevant to resource allocation decisions in a world of rapidly evolving environments. This evolution extends to all types of organizations: securities exchange listed and unlisted businesses, not-for-profits, public sector entities, as well as other entities. Decisions made by professional accountants also reach well beyond resource allocation decisions to, for example, strategic leadership and risk management.

However, many accounting education programs have been slow to embrace recent agents for change. In 1985, Wriston warned:

Accounting education is challenged to keep pace with opportunities and expectations that students learn to think in new ways and develop the necessary skills and knowledge to maintain the profession's ability to meet these evolving opportunities. Without innovation and change, the discipline and profession risk becoming supplanted by technology or possibly rendered irrelevant because of mechanical rules and artificial contrivances.

More than 25 years later, the American Accounting Association (AAA) and the American Institute of Certified Public Accountants (AICPA) collaborated under The Pathways Commission to examine accounting education in the United States. The urgent need for meaningful change is eloquently presented in the Commission's conclusion (p24)[1]:

> Absent a determined, sustained commitment by accounting educators to an educational model that is at the same time broadly formative and comprehensively attuned to the ever-evolving societal demands placed on the accounting profession, the profession faces the very real risk of erosion of its ability to deliver on its commitment to serve the broad public interest associated with reliable accounting information. This eventuality has far-reaching and profound implications, stretching well beyond the bounds of the accounting profession.

The stern warning of the Pathways Commission should not be ignored. PAOs around the globe are currently studying, planning and strategizing how to respond to changes in the business environment and ensure that the accounting profession remains relevant. Some of the greatest changes are happening in the vast area of technology. The Association of Chartered Certified Accountants (ACCA) advises that "The finance function needs to change and adopt new technologies if it is to remain relevant. Finance leaders need to act now if they are to avoid a technology deficit that it will be challenging to overcome."[2]

Adapting to technological change requires technical knowledge and skills, but even more so, it requires competence in strategic thinking, prioritization, risk assessment and change management. This is the underlying foundation for the recent human resources trend focusing more on behavioral skills such as attitude, adaptability, and learning agility than technical skills and experience. This is where CBAETC is most relevant, as it builds competence across a broad range of technical and—more importantly—professional skills, values, ethics, and attitudes that allow professional accountants to thrive in times of uncertainty and rapid change.

By increasing the competence of professional accountants to make, audit, and regulate judgments in preparing financial information, CBAETC enables providing higher quality financial information. Such information increases investor confidence through more informed economic decision-making that, in turn, provides a solid foundation for higher and more sustainable economic growth. But real progress is only possible if organizations are committed to action and not just the appearance of action.

The motivation for transitioning from a knowledge-based approach to a competency-based approach in accounting education can also be linked to the shift from rules-based accounting to principles-based accounting over the last 30 years (figures 1.1 and 1.2).

Principles-based standards involve many levels of judgments that relate to accounting matters. Preparers make initial judgments about uncertain accounting issues. The preparer's judgment may then be evaluated or challenged by auditors, investors, regulators, legal claimants, and others. Critical thinking skills become far more important in this context. The financial statements produced will also support the move from collateral-based lending decisions to lending decisions that are based on the financial performance of the prospective borrower.

This shift to principles-based standards underscores the necessity for organizations to devote attention to moving to CBAETC sooner rather than later, due to the increased need for judgment and flexibility in dealing with uncertainty and complexity in decision-making.

FIGURE 1.1
Rules-based accounting

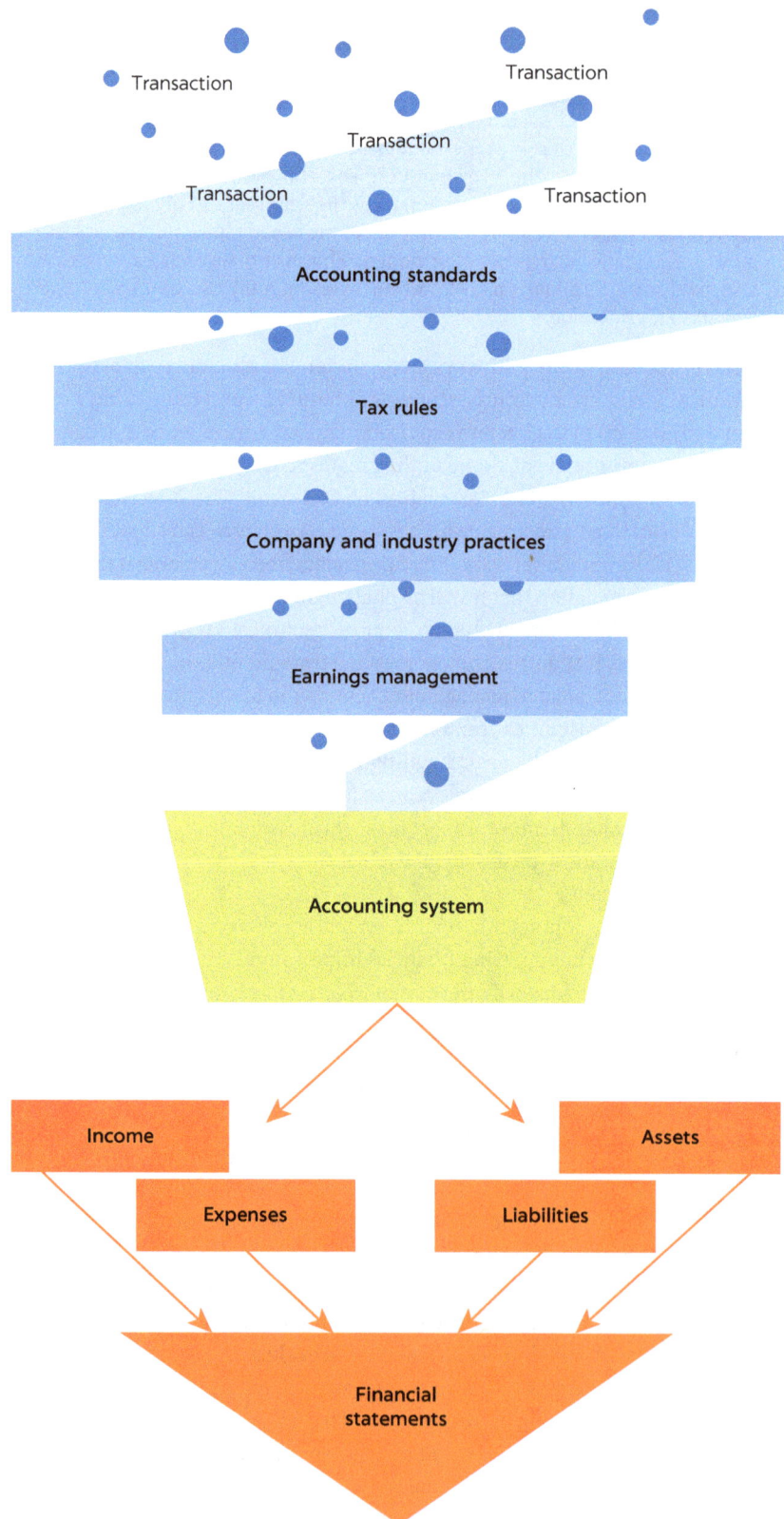

Transaction

Transaction

Transaction

Transaction

Transaction

Accounting standards

Tax rules

Company and industry practices

Earnings management

Accounting system

Income

Assets

Expenses

Liabilities

Financial
statements

FIGURE 1.2

Principles-based accounting

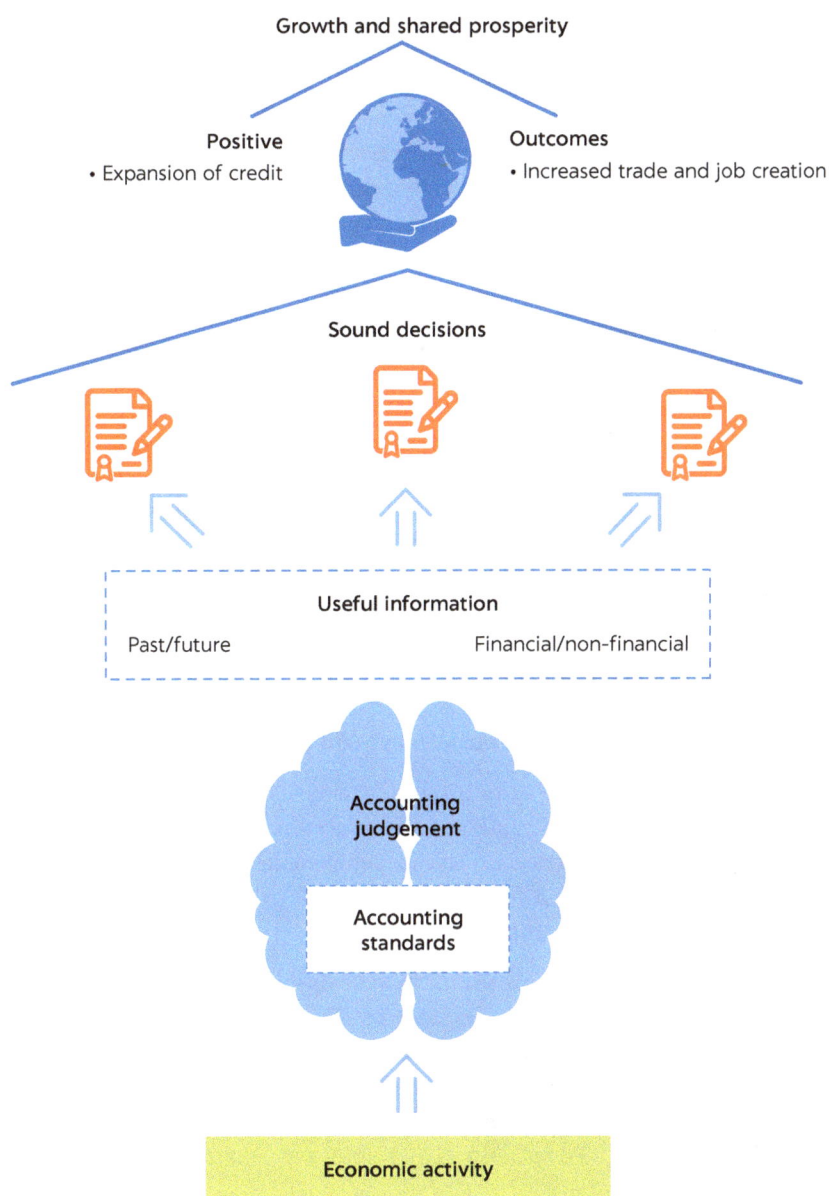

Growth and shared prosperity

Positive
• Expansion of credit

Outcomes
• Increased trade and job creation

Sound decisions

Useful information

Past/future

Financial/non-financial

Accounting
judgement

Accounting
standards

Economic activity

WHAT ARE THE MAIN OUTCOMES AND OUTPUTS OF CBAETC?

Implementing a competency-based approach to education, training, and certification of professional accountants results in the following tangible outcomes
and outputs:

1. **Organizational Vision:** Implementing CBAETC requires that the organization first develop and clearly articulate its mission, strategy, and expected
outcomes so that continuous improvement can be monitored, measured
and reported to stakeholders. With respect to CBAETC, the vision will usually center on serving the public interest by producing and certifying sufficient numbers of competent professional accountants to meet the needs
and expectations of society. More broadly, the vision will generally include

community service and engagement through research and outreach. These in turn require clear articulation of what is needed and expected by the society and communities served.

2. **Competency Framework:** The underpinning of the entire CBAETC approach is a current, relevant, and validated competency framework that clearly identifies and describes the requisite professional competencies and specifies proficiency levels and knowledge topics for each competence area that must be demonstrated by a candidate in order to be certified as a professional accountant.

   This Framework provides a consistent foundation upon which all programs, policies and requirements can be mapped, to ensure that a focus on professional competence is maintained. Development and validation of the Framework requires consultation with regulators and other decision-makers, including stakeholders in the marketplace, such as employers and clients. This consultation plays an important role in not only helping the organization identify its required curriculum, but also forms the basis of valid and relevant assessments that allow the organization to attest to the professional competence of its certified members. Furthermore, stakeholder consultation enables the delineation of relevant competencies for various roles or specialities of professional accountants, as well as a mechanism to ensure implementation "buy-in."

3. **Supporting Competency Maps:** Detailed Competency Maps document the links between the Competency Framework and the more comprehensive formal education and practical experience programs that are designed to give effect to the vision, that is to develop the competence of aspiring professional accountants. More detailed Competency Maps can also help ensure that:

   a. The knowledge, skills, and attributes developed in initial courses of formal education scaffold efficiently and effectively to subsequent more advanced courses and the practical experience component; and
   b. The formal education component and the practical experience component synchronize appropriately.

   *Note that in this Guide, we use the term **Competency Framework** to refer to the overall listing of competency statements by domain, with specified proficiency levels. We use **Competency Map** to refer to a document or series of documents that illustrate the linkages between elements in a professional program of studies and the Competency Framework. In other sources, you may see a Framework referred to as a Competency Map. This important distinction will become clearer later in the Guide.*

4. **Competency-Based Education and Assessment Tools:** For IPD, CBAETC results in producing and continually updating a comprehensive set of education and assessment materials that are appropriate for developing and evaluating the required competence at the appropriate level of proficiency. These materials include, for example, collaborative classroom activities, hands-on simulations, and capstone, multidisciplinary case study-based examinations. Such activities and assessments allow aspiring professional accountants to develop and demonstrate the application of technical knowledge using high-order critical thinking skills and to make appropriate judgments in complex simulations involving real-world facts and circumstances. CBAETC also stresses the need to build and demonstrate proficiency in communicating the relevant outputs with key stakeholders.

   CBAETC for CPD is designed to maintain, enhance and extend the competence of a professional accountant. This includes working towards a specialty, such as auditing, management accounting, or finance. The main outcomes are the same as those for IPD, but the requisite competencies, proficiency levels, and knowledge topics are commensurate with the higher expectations associated with a specialty domain.

In addition to specialties, the Competency Framework provides the scope of topic areas that professional members may consider relevant for CPD.

5. **Enhanced Operational Capacity:** A full implementation of CBAETC results in:

- Educators who are skilled in applying appropriate teaching methods using teaching materials that are designed to progressively foster competence
- Practical experience supervisors who are responsible for overseeing relevant practical workplace experience to defined proficiency levels, and
- Administrators capable of developing and administering policies and programs to effectively support the development and maintenance of professional competence in students, candidates, and members.

Effective operational capacity development in accounting requires the well-coordinated collaboration of PAOs, accounting academia (teaching and research), and accountants in practice.

6. **Enhanced Competence of Professional Accountants:** The overarching purpose of implementing CBAETC is to increase and maintain the competence of professional accountants at both the point of certification and throughout their careers (figure 1.3), to serve the legitimate objectives of their employers and clients while always protecting the public interest.

FIGURE 1.3

Developing competent professional accounts

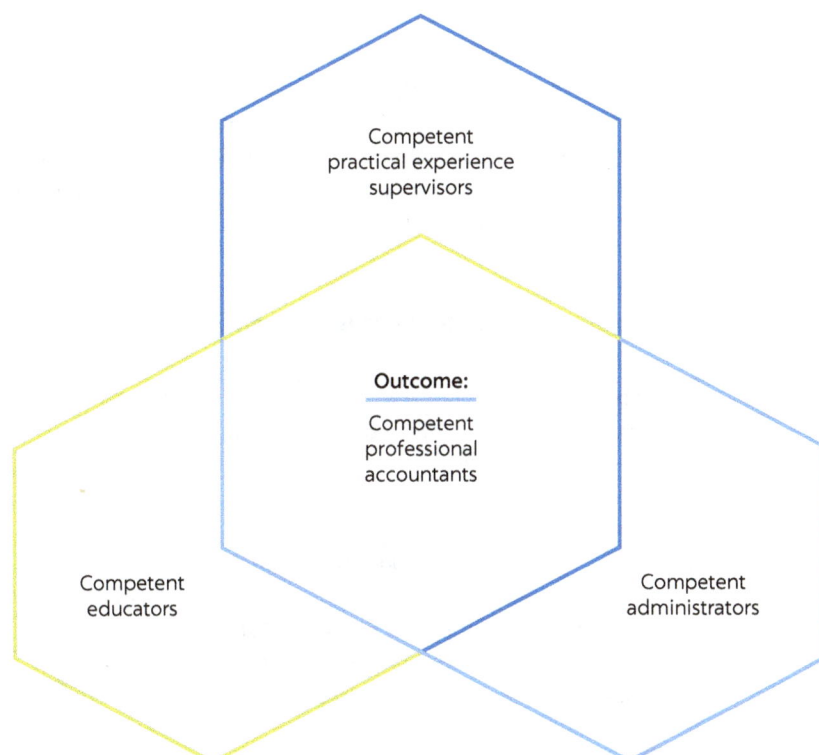

ARE THERE INTERNATIONAL STANDARDS FOR CBAETC?

IAESB's International Education Standards—A key resource for CBAETC

The International Accounting Education Standards Board™ (IAESB) develops education standards, guidance, and information papers for use by member organizations of the International Federation of Accountants® (IFAC), under a shared standard-setting process involving the Public Interest Oversight Board, which oversees the activities of the IAESB, and the IAESB Consultative Advisory Group, which provides public interest input into the development of the standards and guidance. The structures and processes that support the operations of the IAESB are facilitated by IFAC.

The IAESB develops and maintains the International Education Standards (IESs) that serve as a key resource for implementing CBAETC (table 1.2). IFAC requires its member bodies to comply with its Statements of Membership Obligations (SMOs).[3] SMO 2 requires compliance with IESs to the extent that IFAC member organizations have direct responsibility for and authority over this area, and best endeavors for those IFAC member organizations that do not have such authority.

The IESs establish requirements[4] for entry to professional accounting education programs, IPD of aspiring professional accountants, and CPD of professional accountants. For those IESs addressing IPD, each competence area has been assigned a level of proficiency that aspiring professional accountants are expected to achieve by the end of IPD. This level of proficiency indicates the context in which the relevant learning outcomes are expected to be demonstrated at the time of certification.

Professional accountants perform a variety of roles, ranging from corporate controller to specialities such as an audit engagement partner. Consequently, PAOs must determine the competencies and criteria for qualification, certification, or licensure that are appropriate to the professional accountancy roles their members undertake.[5] Some PAOs appropriately adopt learning and development requirements for their members that go beyond those in the IESs. Such changes may be warranted when a PAO prepares professional accountants or aspiring professional accountants to work within a particular industry sector or for a particular role that is a matter of public interest.

TABLE 1.2 **International Education Standards for professional accountants**

	STANDARD	EFFECTIVE DATE
IPD	IES 1 *Entry Requirements to Professional Accounting Education Programs (2014)*	1 July 2014
IPD	IES 2 *Technical Competence (2015)*	1 July 2015
IPD	IES 3 *Professional Skills (2015)*	1 July 2015
IPD	IES 4 *Professional Values Ethics and Attitudes (2015)*	1 July 2015
IPD	IES 5 *Practical Experience (2015)*	1 July 2015
IPD	IES 6 *Assessment of Professional Competence (2015)*	1 July 2015
CPD	IES 7 *Continuing Professional Development (2014)*	1 January 2014
CPD	IES 8 *Professional Competence for Engagement Partners Responsible for Audits of Financial Statements (2016)*	1 July 2016

In addition to these standards, the IAESB offers guidance materials to support implementing a learning outcomes approach to developing competence.[6]

Additional international guidance

In addition to IAESB's requirements and guidance, a benefit of globalization is the ability for PAOs to learn from each other's experience. Such benchmarking enables more rapid implementation of the changes needed for PAOs to move to competency-based accounting education. Good examples of PAO competency maps include those developed and maintained by the Chartered Professional Accountants of Canada (CPA Canada) and the South African Institute of Chartered Accountants (SAICA).[7]

Similarly, it can be most efficient to employ techniques used by others to more effectively attain the mapped competencies. For example, **framework-based teaching** is recommended by the International Accounting Standards Board (the Board) Education Initiative and others to develop IFRS® Standards financial reporting competencies.[8] This approach continually frames and contextualizes the IFRS® Standards requirements being taught within the IFRS *Conceptual Framework*. In other words, rather than just focusing on "what" is required to comply with IFRS when recording and reporting transactions and events, it frames this in the context of the objectives that are being sought to illustrate "why."

> The ability to make reasoned, informed judgments and estimates is crucial to appropriate application of IFRS. Framework-based teaching is the best way to educate students to enable them to make those judgments and estimates. Framework-based teaching helps students understand the objective of and the concepts underlying financial reporting, thereby helping them understand the "why" of IFRS requirements and not just the "how." Understanding the "why" forms the foundation for their ability to make the judgments and estimates necessary to apply IFRS. Framework-based teaching also provides students with long-lasting knowledge of IFRS—requirements in IFRS change with every new standard issued, whereas the concepts underlying IFRS live for decades. This is the approach I use to teach my students and highly recommend it to all teachers of IFRS (Mary Barth, Professor of Accounting, Stanford University).[9]

NOTES

1. The Pathways Commission: Charting a National Strategy for the Next Generation of Accountants (July 2012): 24 (For more information about the Pathways Commission see http://commons.aaahq.org/groups/2d690969a3/summary).
2. Association of Chartered Certified Accountants, The Race for Relevance: Technology Opportunities for the Finance Function, London: ACCA, 2017 at 34.
3. Paragraph 2.3.b of the IFAC Constitution.
4. The IAESB recognizes that individual IFAC member organizations may adopt learning and development requirements that go beyond IESs. (paragraph 36 of the Framework for IESs)
5. Paragraph 41 of the Framework for IESs.
6. The IAESB guidance material is available at https://www.ifac.org/publications-resources/guidance-support-implementation-learning-outcomes-approach
7. SAICA made use of the Canadian Institute of Chartered Accountants' (following a merger with other Canadian PAOs became CPA Canada) earlier work when developing their competency map.

8. Framework-based teaching material "is designed to support IFRS teachers to develop in students the ability to make the judgments that are necessary to apply IFRS and the IFRS for SMEs [small and medium enterprises] and to prepare students for lifelong learning." See:http://www.ifrs.org/Use-around-the-world/Education/Pages/Framework-based -teaching-material.aspx

9. IFRS Foundation, A Guide to the IFRS Education Initiative (December 2015): 3.

REFERENCES

International Federation of Accountants. 2017. *International Standards: 2017 Global Status Report*. New York: IFAC. pp. 4–5.

Wriston, W.B. 1985. "Microseconds and Macropolicy." *AEI Journal on Government and Society* 9 (2, March/April): 13–16.

2

Overview of the CBAETC Journey

This chapter provides a high-level overview of the CBAETC process. This process will be examined in much greater practical detail in Chapter 3.

The journey to CBAETC involves five key stages, as shown in figure 2.1. Although the five stages are sequential, the process should allow for ongoing refinement and iteration of the stages. To respond to the continuing evolution of the accounting services market, stages 1–4 should be repeated every 3–5 years, beginning with a review of the Competency Framework, to reflect the changing needs of stakeholders and the professional environment. In the intervening period, smaller recalibrations might also be appropriate.

Organizations attempting CBAETC for the first time may face resource constraints, and this may impede their ability to implement a fully comprehensive model. To assist these organizations, guidance is provided on condensed approaches that can help an organization make tangible progress towards CBAETC, using significantly fewer resources, as a starting point. This guidance is provided in Chapter 3, in the detailed discussion of each stage.

FIGURE 2.1

The five stages of the CBAETC journey

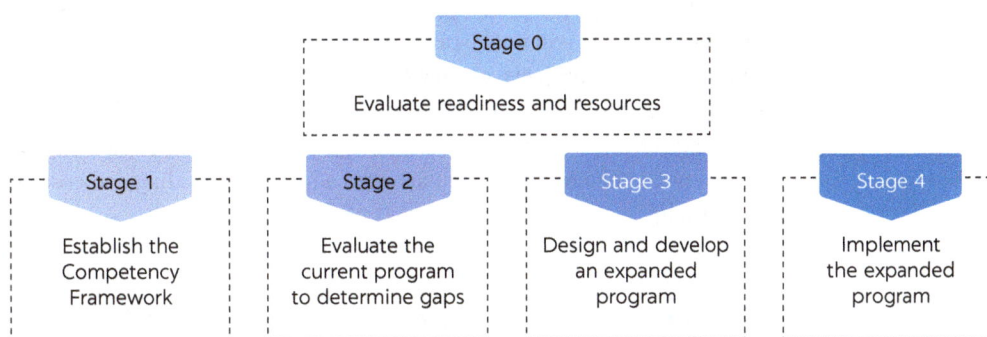

STAGE 0: EVALUATE READINESS AND RESOURCES

Review the local regulatory environment governing the profession within the jurisdiction, and assess the financial and human resources able to be sourced and allocated to CBAETC.

Why is this stage necessary?

Implementing CBAETC requires commitment on the part of all stakeholders in the jurisdiction who have responsibility and authority over educating and training professional accountants. It is important to understand up front the regulatory systems that will impact implementation and the stakeholders driving the need and opportunities for CBAETC. Similarly, it is essential that the organization develop a clear picture at the outset as to the level of funding that will be available, and the current availability of capable educators, administrators, and work supervisors to include in the project.

What will we have achieved when we've completed stage 0?

You will have a clear understanding of your current environment in terms of regulation and business trends, and will know how these will impact your implementation of CBAETC. You will also have determined the financial and human resources available to the project, which will help with ongoing budgeting and prioritization.

How do we get there?

The purpose of Stage 0 is to undertake the pre-requisite research and analysis to set the project up for success (figure 2.2). It is important for the organization to understand the regulatory and authority structures overseeing the profession, and that collaborations with other stakeholders with authority begin as early as possible. Similarly, the organization should gather information on the financial and human resources available for CBAETC, in order to commence budgeting and prioritization. Priorities can be set based on a high-level read of this document by key project sponsors and contributors, particularly Chapter 2.

At this stage, budgets will not be precise. Costs are invariably difficult to estimate on these types of projects, as they differ drastically between jurisdictions based on priorities, the maturity of the existing education system, local economic factors, the extent that international consultants will be needed, to name a few. Budgets will need to be revisited regularly and adjusted as funding and costing estimates firm up.

STAGE 1: ESTABLISH THE COMPETENCY FRAMEWORK

Establish the competencies and proficiency levels that newly-certified members of the PAO (or equivalent body) should possess to serve client and employer needs in the domestic context, and the knowledge topics that support the competencies.

FIGURE 2.2

The three steps of Stage 0

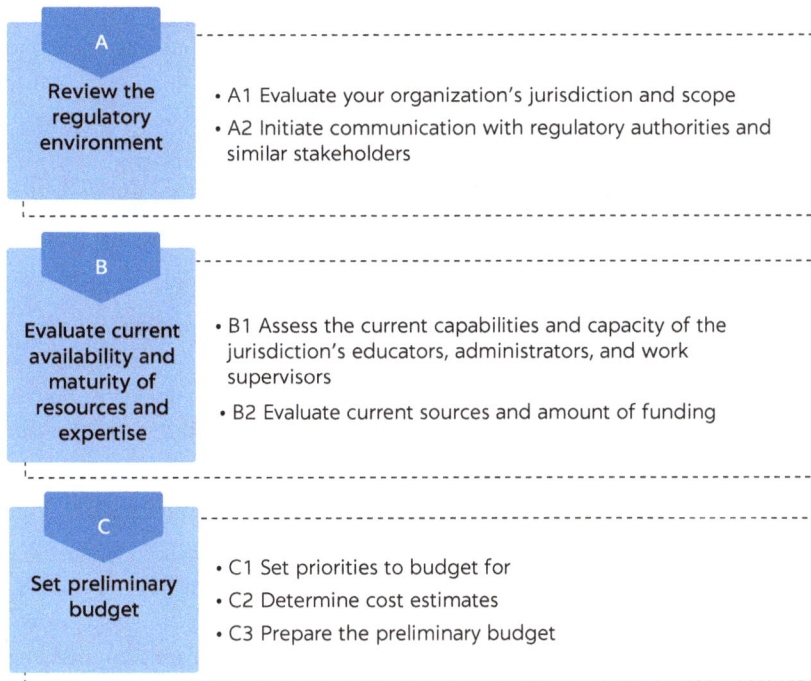

| A — Review the regulatory environment | • A1 Evaluate your organization's jurisdiction and scope
• A2 Initiate communication with regulatory authorities and similar stakeholders |

| B — Evaluate current availability and maturity of resources and expertise | • B1 Assess the current capabilities and capacity of the jurisdiction's educators, administrators, and work supervisors
• B2 Evaluate current sources and amount of funding |

| C — Set preliminary budget | • C1 Set priorities to budget for
• C2 Determine cost estimates
• C3 Prepare the preliminary budget |

Why is this stage necessary?

In order to successfully develop and assess the competence of accounting professionals and students, it is necessary to specify a comprehensive and clear set of competency statements and requisite proficiency levels, along with the knowledge topics that support competence. This Competency Framework is used as the basis for designing program elements to ensure the full range of competencies are developed and evaluated during the certification program. It serves as the central document against which all program elements are mapped to facilitate updating and ensuring consistency throughout the program.

Similarly, with respect to Content for professional development (CPD), the Competency Framework sets the scope of what should be considered relevant CPD, and guides the development of CPD courses for members following certification (e.g., career advancement or specialization). Without a Framework, programs will tend to be poorly aligned, or may have inconsistencies, unintended omissions, and or inefficient overlaps.

What will we have achieved when we've completed stage 1?

You will have developed a fully-validated Competency Framework that includes:

- A number of competency domains to provide structure to the Framework
- A complete set of competency statements that encompasses the role of a professional accountant in your jurisdiction
- Designated proficiency levels for each statement, based on the role
- Sets of knowledge topics to support each competency domain or statement.

This Competency Framework will serve as the standard against which you map and evaluate your current program elements in Stage 2.

> It is the identification of high level competencies which will inform the academic, training, and assessment programs, and enable appropriate content, emphases, and teaching and learning strategies to be developed."
>
> —SAICA[1]

How do we get there?

This stage (figure 2.3) involves research, analysis, consultation, and distillation. The research phase typically includes:

- Reviewing the business and professional trends affecting, or likely to affect, the services domestic professional accountants provide
- Reviewing the Competency Frameworks of leading PAOs from other jurisdictions to understand the competencies they require their members to demonstrate; and
- Undertaking initial, targeted, primary stakeholder consultations such as interviews and focus groups.

The research results are analyzed considering all relevant factors, and distilled into preliminary findings of the core competencies that domestic professional accountants should demonstrate. Those competencies are compiled in a draft Competency Framework.

Broad-based domestic consultation—often termed a Practice Analysis—is then undertaken with a wide variety of stakeholders both internal and external to the profession. The Practice Analysis uses comprehensive surveys and focus groups to test the validity of the competency domains and statements identified, inform the level of proficiency appropriate for each competency statement, and develop a list of underlying knowledge topics. A Practice Analysis likely requires use of experienced international experts to train and mentor those charged with developing the Competency Framework.

The results of the Practice Analysis are used to refine and finalize the proposed Competency Framework.

STAGE 2: EVALUATE THE CURRENT PROGRAM TO DETERMINE GAPS

Review the existing program elements and evaluate the current level of competence among practicing professionals, to establish gaps from the desired competence levels.

Why is this stage necessary?

Your Competency Framework provides a clear picture of the knowledge, skills, and attributes expected of professional accountants in your jurisdiction. Your current programs most likely will not fully support the Competency Framework, and will need expanding, revising and augmenting. Before embarking on developing new program elements for IPD or CPD, however, it is essential that you fully understand which current program elements should be retained and to what extent the Framework is being covered, to maximize your efficiency and help you allocate resources most effectively. Without adequate evaluation and

FIGURE 2.3

The three steps of Stage 1

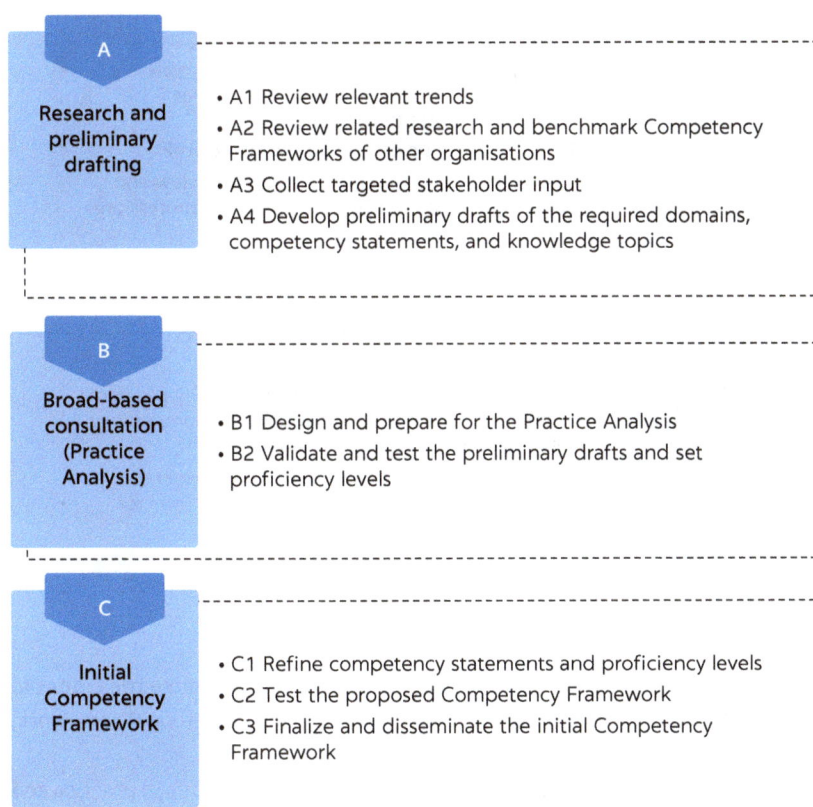

A	
Research and preliminary drafting	• A1 Review relevant trends • A2 Review related research and benchmark Competency Frameworks of other organisations • A3 Collect targeted stakeholder input • A4 Develop preliminary drafts of the required domains, competency statements, and knowledge topics
B	
Broad-based consultation (Practice Analysis)	• B1 Design and prepare for the Practice Analysis • B2 Validate and test the preliminary drafts and set proficiency levels
C	
Initial Competency Framework	• C1 Refine competency statements and proficiency levels • C2 Test the proposed Competency Framework • C3 Finalize and disseminate the initial Competency Framework

mapping of the current program, you risk eliminating current resources that are valuable, or continuing to rely on elements that do not support your pursuit of competence development at given proficiency levels.

What will we have achieved when we've completed stage 2?

You will have:

- Identified all of the program elements that are currently in use to educate and train professional accountants in your jurisdiction
- Mapped all existing program elements (e.g., education, evaluation, experience, CPD) to the Competency Framework
- Determined gaps in coverage of competency statements at expected proficiency levels within the certification program
- determined gaps in the competence of current professional accountants.

The maps and gap analyses will guide your development of new program elements in Stage 3 (including IPD and CPD).

How do we get there?

In this stage, (figure 2.4) key stakeholders inside and outside of the profession are consulted to:

1. Review the current certification program elements (e.g., education curricula and syllabi, exam blueprints, practical experience requirements, CPD

FIGURE 2.4

The two steps of Stage 2

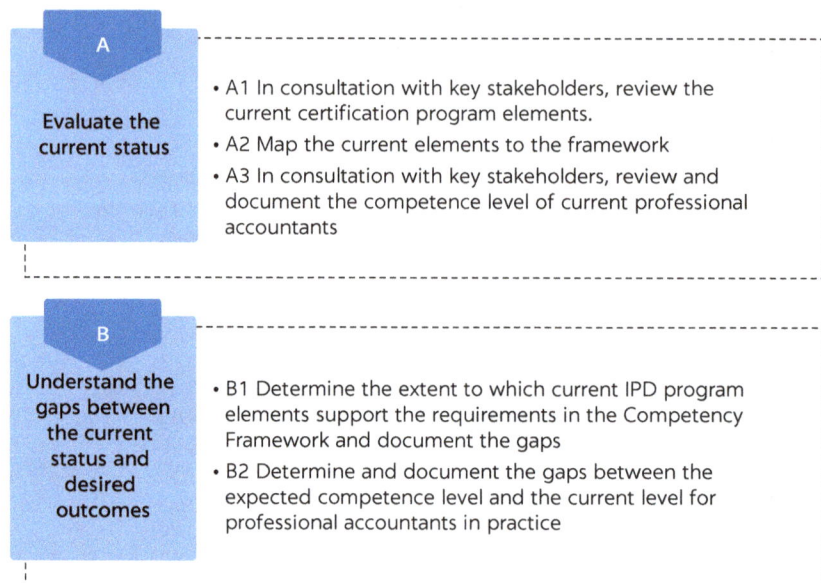

A

Evaluate the current status

- A1 In consultation with key stakeholders, review the current certification program elements.
- A2 Map the current elements to the framework
- A3 In consultation with key stakeholders, review and document the competence level of current professional accountants

B

Understand the gaps between the current status and desired outcomes

- B1 Determine the extent to which current IPD program elements support the requirements in the Competency Framework and document the gaps
- B2 Determine and document the gaps between the expected competence level and the current level for professional accountants in practice

requirements) and map these to the Framework to determine the extent to which they can reasonably be expected to support the Competency Framework, and

2. Examine the current competence of professional accountants in practice and identify the gaps between the current state of how and to what level professional accountants are trained and evaluated, and the desired state as documented in the Competency Framework.

In Stage 3, gaps in the education and experience elements of the program will be resolved through the development of new/expanded IPD program elements, while gaps in the current competence of practicing professionals will be addressed through CPD.

STAGE 3: DESIGN AND DEVELOP AN EXPANDED PROGRAM

Based on the gap analysis in Stage 2:

- Design an expanded program that incorporates existing program elements as appropriate
- Develop and map new education, training and assessment elements and/or accreditation policies to adequately cover the Competency Framework, and
- Revise/enhance CPD requirements and options to address gaps in the competence of existing members.

Why is this stage necessary?

Once you have determined the gaps in the current program elements, you need to determine the most efficient and effective way to close those gaps, both in the education and training program for IPD, and with respect to current deficiencies in the competence of practicing professionals. This may include accrediting tertiary-level educational institutions and/or training institutions if they are relied on as a primary source of professional accounting education.

What will we have achieved when we've completed stage 3?

You will have a clearly defined scope of the new elements to be developed. This will include determining, as appropriate based on the scope, an overall design for the:

- New program for education and exams
- New training requirements; and
- New CPD requirements.

You will also have created and mapped to the Competency Framework:

- Newly-developed education program elements to develop and assess competence
- Updated accreditation policies for tertiary-level education providers
- Newly-developed training program elements to develop and assess competence; and
- Newly-developed CPD program elements to help close competence gaps in existing professionals.

How do we get there?

The magnitude of the gap between the desired state (as documented in the Competency Framework) and the current state determines the effort needed and the time required to design and develop the expanded program (figure 2.5). The time range also reflects the uncertainty of resources available for this process.

In cases where the gaps determined indicate that significant change is needed, capacity building likely requires use of international experts experienced in CBAETC to train and mentor those charged with designing and developing new elements.

Design

In addition to the size of gaps between the current and the desired state, there are other practical questions that need to be answered that will impact the scope of the expanded program:

- What is the jurisdiction of the organization to effect change?
- What resources and funding opportunities are available?
- What other constraints may impede progress?

An important first step in the design process is to establish the boundaries for what can and cannot be done within the constraints identified. Working within the constraints, and/or collaborating with other organizations to gain additional breadth of authority and resources, new elements of education, training and CPD programs are designed to fill gaps noted in Stage 2.

The design of the new expanded program should include a plan of which competencies should be covered and in which program elements along a continuum,

FIGURE 2.5
The four steps of Stage 3

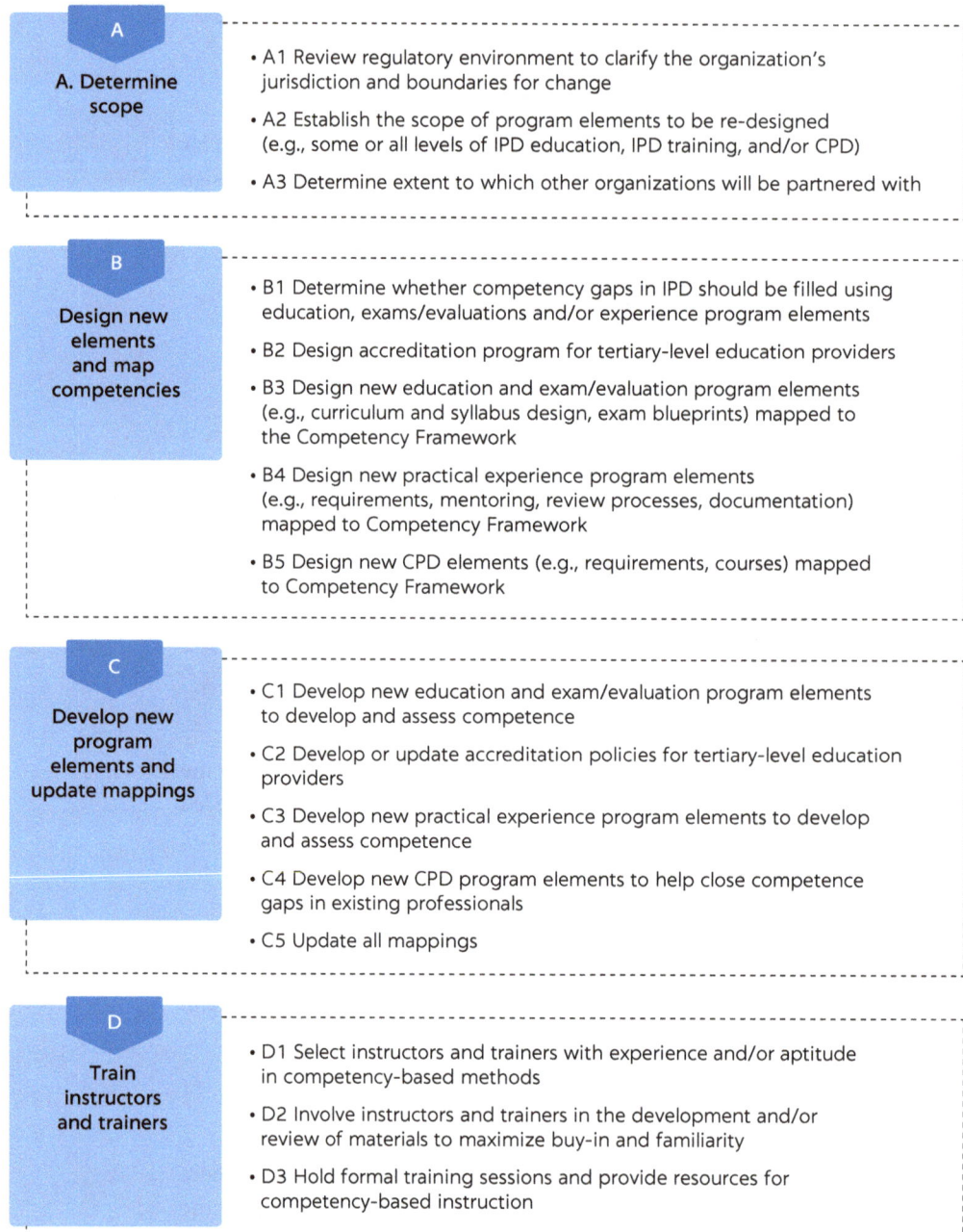

A

A. Determine scope

- A1 Review regulatory environment to clarify the organization's jurisdiction and boundaries for change
- A2 Establish the scope of program elements to be re-designed (e.g., some or all levels of IPD education, IPD training, and/or CPD)
- A3 Determine extent to which other organizations will be partnered with

B

Design new elements and map competencies

- B1 Determine whether competency gaps in IPD should be filled using education, exams/evaluations and/or experience program elements
- B2 Design accreditation program for tertiary-level education providers
- B3 Design new education and exam/evaluation program elements (e.g., curriculum and syllabus design, exam blueprints) mapped to the Competency Framework
- B4 Design new practical experience program elements (e.g., requirements, mentoring, review processes, documentation) mapped to Competency Framework
- B5 Design new CPD elements (e.g., requirements, courses) mapped to Competency Framework

C

Develop new program elements and update mappings

- C1 Develop new education and exam/evaluation program elements to develop and assess competence
- C2 Develop or update accreditation policies for tertiary-level education providers
- C3 Develop new practical experience program elements to develop and assess competence
- C4 Develop new CPD program elements to help close competence gaps in existing professionals
- C5 Update all mappings

D

Train instructors and trainers

- D1 Select instructors and trainers with experience and/or aptitude in competency-based methods
- D2 Involve instructors and trainers in the development and/or review of materials to maximize buy-in and familiarity
- D3 Hold formal training sessions and provide resources for competency-based instruction

to ensure alignment and comprehensive coverage. For example, which competencies are expected to be developed and assessed during the education program, and which are primarily covered during practical experience? It is also important that sufficient overlap or redundancy in competency coverage be built in to the program elements to ensure reliability, but that elements are focused on specific sets of competencies in a progressive manner. The need to balance efficiency and effectiveness dictates that not all competencies can (or should) be covered in each course, and a logical progression and delineation needs to be designed into the program before education, evaluation, training and CPD elements are developed.

Development

Once the design of the elements has been laid out in terms of curricula, syllabi, evaluation blueprints, training and CPD program specifications etc., the elements are developed, paying close attention to the competencies required to be covered in each element, and their expected proficiency levels. In most cases, this involves redesigning:

- IPD and CPD courses and their delivery mediums to develop competencies as designed
- Practical experience requirements and their administration—to foster the development of competence to the required proficiency levels; and
- IPD (and possibly CPD) assessments that certify attaining the relevant competence.

Throughout this process, it is essential that all new elements are aligned and mapped to the Competency Framework.

Designing and developing an expanded program requires a set of properly coordinated actions, with clearly designated responsibilities, and carefully managed collaboration and oversight to ensure requirements are met and mappings are updated.

Coordination is particularly important when PAOs outsource to others (for example, to universities) some or all of the formal education component of IPD, CPD specializations, or both. All providers of formal education must clearly understand the competencies and associated proficiency levels that the PAO expects their graduates to have attained to receive advanced standing toward designation.

STAGE 4: IMPLEMENT THE EXPANDED PROGRAM

Take the actions necessary to properly implement the new program elements in education, evaluation, training and CPD. This includes setting timelines, deploying resources, and evaluating results.

Why is this stage necessary?

Newly-designed and developed program elements need to be carefully implemented by people with sufficient experience to make them successful. Without careful planning, resource allocation, monitoring and evaluation of the first offerings of new elements, small issues can lead to frustration for participants, resulting in the benefits of CBAETC not being fully realized.

What will we have achieved when we've completed stage 4?

You will have piloted an initial offering of all new program elements, and will have compiled lessons learned. You will have documented a plan for future refinements to program elements and updated the Competency Map as needed.

How do we get there?

This final stage is the culmination of the project (figure 2.6). Initial offerings of new program elements are run, with careful monitoring and collaboration. It

FIGURE 2.6

The three steps of Stage 4

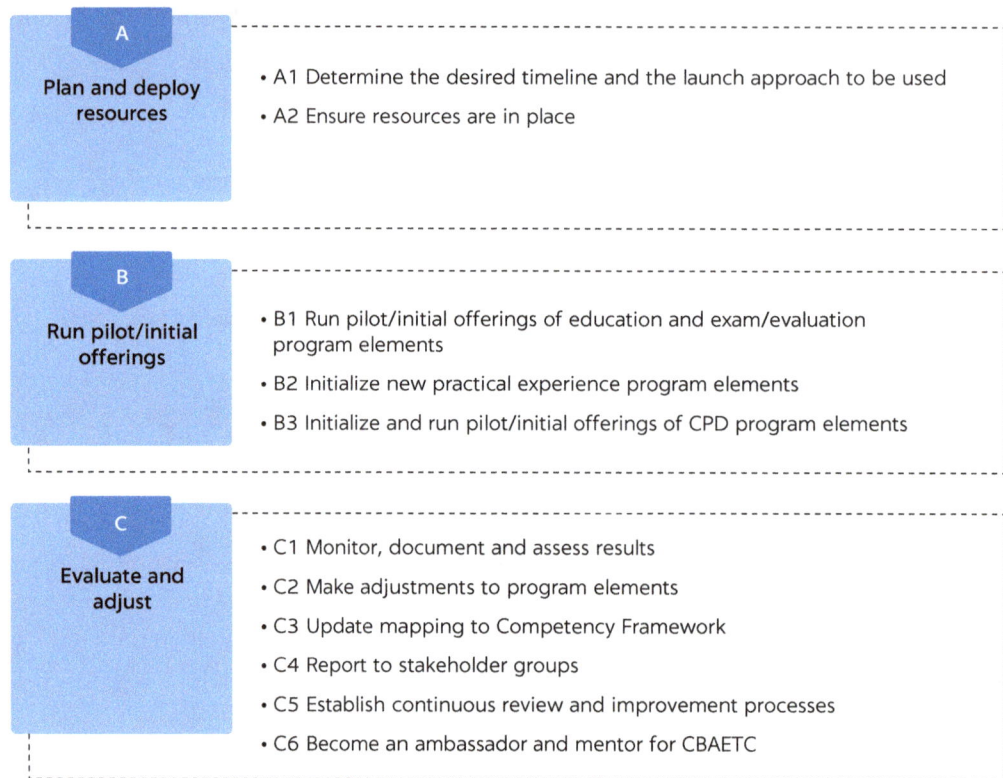

A

Plan and deploy resources

- A1 Determine the desired timeline and the launch approach to be used
- A2 Ensure resources are in place

B

Run pilot/initial offerings

- B1 Run pilot/initial offerings of education and exam/evaluation program elements
- B2 Initialize new practical experience program elements
- B3 Initialize and run pilot/initial offerings of CPD program elements

C

Evaluate and adjust

- C1 Monitor, document and assess results
- C2 Make adjustments to program elements
- C3 Update mapping to Competency Framework
- C4 Report to stakeholder groups
- C5 Establish continuous review and improvement processes
- C6 Become an ambassador and mentor for CBAETC

is essential to ensure instructors and trainers are adequately supported during the first offerings to gain as much feedback as possible for future improvements. No program elements should be expected to be flawless the first time they are offered.

Once findings from the first round of offerings have been obtained and analyzed, and additional plans developed for further refinements to the program, it is important to report back to key stakeholder groups about progress made and next steps. Less formal, ongoing communication with various stakeholders throughout all stages is, of course, valuable as a normal mechanism of change management.

This Guide aims to support PAOs and others to transition from a knowledge-based approach to CBAETC. Doing so fosters the critical thinking skills that are fundamental to modern financial information designed to enable more informed economic decision-making and thereby provide a firmer foundation for higher and more sustainable economic growth. Further detail on each of the four key stages follows.

NOTE

1. SAICA's Detailed Guidance for the Academic Programmed: Competencies of a CA(SA) at the point of the Initial Test of Competence (assessment of core technical knowledge) (2014) p4.

The Four Stages of the CBAETC Journey

This chapter provides in-depth practical application guidance of the stages outlined in chapter 2, to be used during the actual implementation of CBAETC. For each stage, guidance is first given on the comprehensive approach to implementing CBAETC. At the end of Stages 1 through 4, a condensed approach is also presented that may serve as a starting point where significant time or other resource limitations do not permit implementing the comprehensive approach. Throughout the stages, watch for highlights of key reference tools and who should be involved.

For each of these stages, your organization should evaluate its available internal resources and expertise and determine to what extent external consultants with international experience in these areas should be engaged.

A WORD ON TERMINOLOGY AND APPROACHES

When implementing CBAETC, your research will inevitably lead you to a variety of approaches and ways of describing concepts. Keep in mind that there are many ways to pursue and implement CBAETC, and the range of resources available will present different scopes, priorities, and methodologies. A solid understanding of the theory and principles behind CBAETC will enable you to work with—and benefit from—a broad range of resources and incorporate relevant learning into your own initiatives.

STAGE 0: EVALUATE READINESS AND RESOURCES

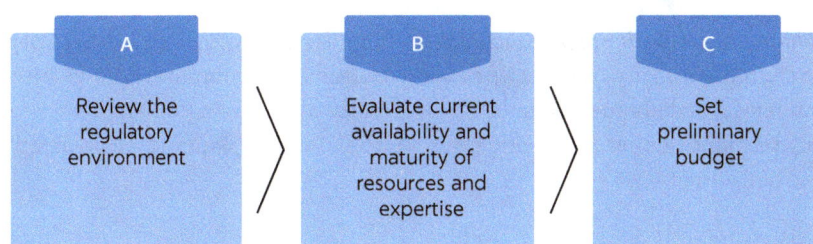

A	B	C
Review the regulatory environment	Evaluate current availability and maturity of resources and expertise	Set preliminary budget

This pre-requisite research and analysis will answer questions regarding the boundaries of authority, resources available, and priorities to be budgeted for. Gain as much clarity as you can in this point, but recognize that you are dealing with imperfect information and that decisions and assumptions will need to be revisited as more information becomes available.

A. Review the regulatory environment

A1. Evaluate your organization's jurisdiction and scope

Determine the boundaries of your authority. CBAETC represents significant change to accounting education and certification requirements. Does your organization have sufficient authority to enact the necessary changes, or are there boundaries that need to be respected?

For example, some PAOs have authority to set professional certification requirements directly, whereas in other jurisdictions, certification requirements are mandated by the government. Similarly, within universities, there may be a greater or lesser extent to which the institution can set curricula and syllabi without state approval.

A key resource for PAOs aiming to establish or advance their public policy efforts and encourage adoption of best practices is the IFAC PAO Development Committee's publication *Finding Your Voice: PAOs, Advocacy, and Public Policy*.

Determine stakeholders with shared authority and/or influence. If your organization does not have sole authority to enact changes in the education and training requirements of professional accountants in your jurisdiction, identify the other stakeholders (i.e., regulators, other PAOs, other standard setters or oversight bodies) who will need to be collaborated with. Additionally, determine stakeholders who are influential in the profession (regardless of whether they have authority). These influencers will be important allies for change.

A2. Initiate communication with regulatory authorities and other stakeholders

Communicate with regulators. If changes need to be implemented in the legal framework for certifying professional accountants and/or specializations (such as auditors) before CBAETC can be undertaken, communication and collaboration with regulatory authorities is essential before proceeding. If, on the other hand, your organization has sole authority over certification requirements, then communications with stakeholders—such as government ministries and other regulators—will be more focused on engaging them in collaboration and starting to generate awareness and buy-in for the coming changes.

Communicate with other stakeholders. Whether your organization has sole or shared authority over certification requirements, communications with influential stakeholders should begin as early as possible, to help generate buy-in, and to gather information that will be useful in planning, prioritizing, and budgeting.

B. Evaluate current availability and maturity of resources and expertise

B1. Assess the current capabilities and capacity of the jurisdiction's educators, administrators, and work supervisors

Survey universities to determine the current familiarity and experience with competency-based education. Within the university system, there are often professors and instructors who are more familiar than others with developing, delivering, and administering competency-based education elements. Surveying well-established universities can lead to development of an "inventory" of individuals with greater capabilities and interest in CBAETC.

Survey training institutions/tuition providers to determine the current familiarity and experience with competency-based education. Similar to university programs, instructors in training institutions may have experience in competency-based education, particularly in those programs that have a practical, task-based focus.

Survey firms and other key employers to determine the current familiarity and experience with competency-based training and workplace evaluation. Larger organizations, particularly those operating internationally, will often have training programs that are designed to provide on-the-job practical instruction for employees. By their nature, these tend to be competency-based (as opposed to focusing on theory).

Based on capabilities, determine capacity. Once you have a clear picture of where capable individuals are currently working, determine if they have excess capacity to devote to CBAETC, or whether they could be seconded to the project of implementing CBAETC.

B2. Evaluate current sources and amount of funding

Determine current funding available within the organization. CBAETC would typically fall within an organization's education budget, but the significance of undertaking CBAETC for the first time means that the typical operational budget for education will likely not be sufficient. Depending on the funding model of the organization, there may be an ability to allocate additional budget to cover CBAETC activities. Often, however, external funding sources will be needed.

Determine current funding available from external sources. If internal funding is insufficient, the organization will need to secure additional funding. Potential sources that can be explored include:

- Grants from local/national government
- Partnering arrangements available with firms and other employers (using the survey information on where capable individuals are located)
- Partnering arrangements with universities or other training institutions (using the survey information on where capable individuals are located)
- Volunteer time from experienced members
- Donor assistance, through international organizations.

C. Set preliminary budget

C1. Set priorities to budget for

Review the CBAETC process and decide which elements will lead to the most meaningful gains. Depending on the current environment in your jurisdiction, you may determine that the greatest gains can be achieved by focusing on certain aspects of the education program, or by putting greater emphasis on competency-based training in the workplace. These decisions will shape your priorities when determining how to allocate limited resources.

Prioritize CBAETC activities. Depending on the current capabilities of individuals discovered in B1, and the relative level of funding available, you will need to set priorities as to where to focus. This exercise will help you decide where you may need to (or want to) use a condensed approach and where you are able to implement CBAETC more fully.

C2. Determine cost estimates

Estimate costs of internal resources. Based on the priorities set and the capabilities determined, estimate the costs of internal resources required to support CBAETC implementation. This should include costs to bring in temporary assistance to free up time for the experienced team who will be directly involved in the implementation.

Estimate costs of external assistance. In addition to internal resources, you will likely need to call on external assistance in the form of individuals with experience who are in academia or training providers, in firms, or in other organizations. If it is determined that local expertise is insufficient to implement the priorities, you will need to hire additional external consultants. Organizations such as the World Bank's CFRR can provide guidance on consulting rates in various jurisdictions.

C3. Prepare the preliminary budget

Based on the available resources (internal and external) and the cost estimates for priorities, develop a preliminary budget. Developing the preliminary budget will require an iterative approach as information is gathered and refined regarding resources, priorities, and costs.

Set a plan to review and update the budget regularly. As CBAETC is undertaken, priorities will likely change as new opportunities and constraints are uncovered. Plan to revise the budget regularly to make the most efficient use of funding that is secured.

STAGE 1: ESTABLISH THE COMPETENCY FRAMEWORK

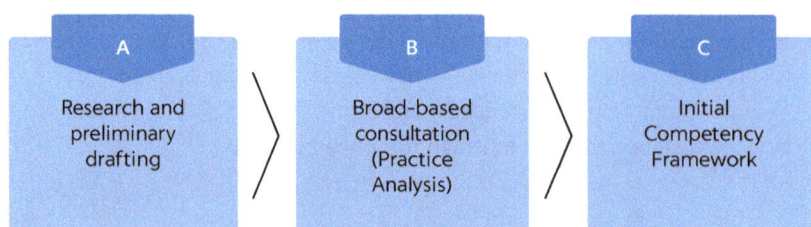

A	B	C
Research and preliminary drafting	Broad-based consultation (Practice Analysis)	Initial Competency Framework

As previously discussed, a Competency Framework identifies and describes the professional competencies that a PAO asserts its newly-certified professional accountant members can demonstrate at specified levels of proficiency.

Your Competency Framework will serve as the foundation that ties together all elements of your programs for members and students by:

- Supporting internal education and professional development programs at both pre- and post-certification
- Defining requirements with respect to competence and expected behaviour to support ethics and disciplinary processes
- Providing a basis for evaluating and granting credit or exemptions for prior studies and work experience for mature students and career-changers wishing to enter the program
- Supporting compliance with national, regional, and international requirements and expectations; and
- Supporting comparisons with other organizations, such as potential partners (e.g., other PAOs; tertiary education institutions; or the governing bodies of other, related professions).

A Competency Framework typically includes the elements indicated in figure 3.1.

Developing the initial Competency Framework for an organisation focuses on establishing the domains (or subject areas); the competency statements comprising each domain and their related levels of proficiency; and the knowledge topics that underlie each competency statement.

Consistent with IESs, PAOs typically specify three proficiency levels that relate to working environments characterized by progressively higher levels of ambiguity, complexity, and uncertainty (table 3.1).

Proficiency levels are generally specified at the point of certification or licensing as a professional accountant, but they can also be set at interim points, such as on entry to a professional program, or on completion of stages within a program. For an example of this approach from CPA Canada, see appendix B.

FIGURE 3.1

Competency Framework

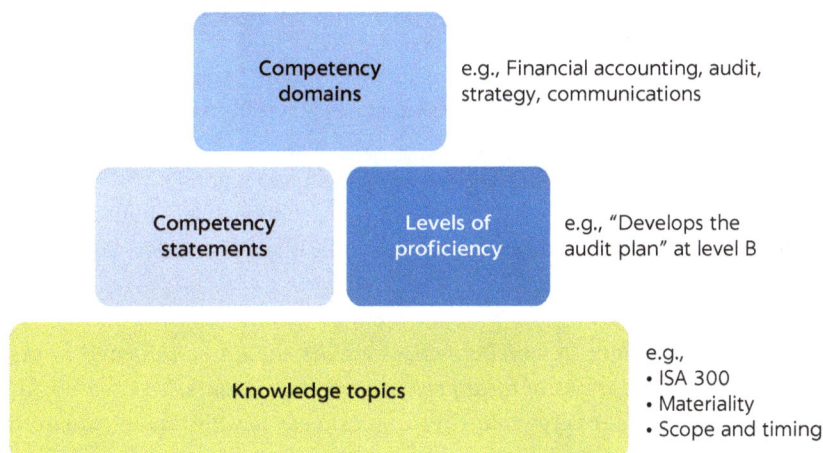

TABLE 3.1 **Proficiency levels**

	FOUNDATION	INTERMEDIATE	ADVANCED
Common verbs used in competency statements/ learning outcomes	Define, describe, explain, summarize, solve (simple tasks)	Apply, analyze, decide, evaluate, interpret	Assess, research, integrate, evaluate, make judgments and resolve or make recommendations
Work environment levels of ambiguity, complexity, and uncertainty	Low	moderate	high

Source: Adapted from IFAC 2015.

If your organization is a PAO that licenses one or more specializations (e.g., audit professionals), you may decide to develop separate Competency Frameworks for each specialty or—more typically—you may use the same Framework, but vary the proficiency levels by specialization (e.g., by raising the proficiency required in financial accounting and audit as an audit licensure requirement). As a key resource, remember that IES 8 addresses *Professional Competence for Engagement Partners Responsible for Audits of Financial Statements.*

A. Research and preliminary drafting

To develop a Competency Framework, you must first understand the environment in which your members work.

A1. Review relevant trends
Evaluate the current, imminent, and likely future trends impacting the business world. Business and professional accounting are evolving quickly. Some trends you'll need to consider include:

- Technological changes, such as software and systems, artificial intelligence, cryptocurrencies and block chain, cloud computing, and data analytics.

    For example, digital barcode scanners that capture goods moving in and out of a business or digitized cards that enable instantaneous, contactless payment. These technologies are becoming an integrated part of everyday life in the technologically advanced, urbanized centers in which we live.
- Globalization.

    Consider, for example, the expectations for professional accountants to support multinational organizations and assist with strategic planning.
- Communication changes, such as social media and the reliance on email and text messaging.

    For example, the power that consumers now have to engage directly with companies, and the reputational risk that can result from even one unhappy and vocal customer.
- Increased expectations for transparency and ethical actions.

    For example, the growth of corporate social responsibility initiatives and the expectation for organizations to meet obligations to broader stakeholder communities.

Determine the extent to which business trends should be reflected in the competency expectations of local professional accountants. To ensure your members are capable of providing the services needed by the market, you need to ensure the competencies you develop are responsive to the changing professional environment. Failure to do so renders members and students redundant and impedes their ability to foster domestic economic growth. At the same time, you need to ensure that the expectations set for professionals and students in your jurisdiction are realistic in the local context.

> Today's students are the future of our profession. We need to educate them for the world they will live in, not the world we lived in. Their world is global. (Barth 2008)

A2. Review related research and benchmark Competency Frameworks of other organizations

Determine if a recent World Bank Report on the Observance of Standards and Codes in Accounting and Auditing (ROSC A&A) exists for your jurisdiction. A ROSC A&A[1] uses the findings of a diagnostic review to provide an assessment of a jurisdiction's accounting, financial reporting, and auditing requirements and practices. It also offers areas for consideration with a view to improving the jurisdiction's institutional environment for corporate financial reporting.

For example, read the extract below from the June 2015 Republic of Serbia ROSC A&A Update:

> Accounting education needs more focus on practical application of IFRS and other standards. Many financial reporting professionals have not yet fully absorbed and learned to apply the modern accounting and auditing standards that Serbia has adopted. Current university curricula could be improved to better assure adequate preparation of accounting students in IFRS, particularly at the undergraduate level. Teaching materials sometimes inadequately address issues of practical application. Moreover, as is the case in many countries, there is inadequate cooperation and linkage between university educators and professional accounting organizations or major accounting firms to assure that university education adequately prepares students to enter the accounting and auditing professions Republic of Serbia ROSC A&A Update.[2]

If you were implementing CBAETC in Serbia, you'd want to ensure that the Competency Framework you develop has strong coverage of interpreting and applying IFRS and other relevant international standards across the range of expected practice, and that the proficiency level for applying IFRS is at the highest level for the complexity of transactions and events that a professional accountant would be expected to face. When it came time to map current elements, you'd expect to see gaps between the levels being currently achieved and the expected levels, and you'd need to design education and experience requirements to close those gaps.

Study the IAESB's IESs. A key reference that will be relevant to every jurisdiction is the IAESB's IESs, discussed in Chapter 1. Specifically, IESs 2, 3, and 4 specify Learning Outcomes expected of all professional accountants with respect to technical competence, professional skills and professional values, ethics, and attitudes.

For example, IES 2 specifies Learning Outcomes in the "Financial accounting and reporting" domain that include:

- Apply IFRS® Standards or other relevant standards to transactions and other events
- Interpret financial statements and related disclosures.

Similarly, IES 4 includes a domain entitled "Professional skepticism and professional judgment," and one of the competency statements in that domain is

"Apply a questioning mindset critically to assess financial information and other relevant data."

Because most PAOs are—or aspire to be—IFAC members, it is essential that these Learning Outcomes be considered and encompassed within an organization's Competency Framework. See appendix B for further guidance on using the IESs during CBAETC.

Review the International Ethics Standards Board for Accountants® (IESBA®) International Code of Ethics for Professional Accountants™ or your local code of ethics. Strong familiarity with the ethics requirements and professional expectations in your jurisdiction will help you ensure that these requirements and expectations are adequately reflected in the Competency Framework.

Review benchmark Competency Frameworks. In this globalized world, you are never alone. Virtually all jurisdictions, albeit to different degrees, are grappling with similar issues in accounting education, training, and certification. Consequently, it is efficient to review and learn from the experience of others when embarking on the CBAETC journey.

As mentioned in Chapter 1, for good practice examples of competency frameworks developed by PAOs in different economies, see, for example, CPA Canada's Competency Map[3] and the Competency Framework of the South African Institute of CAs (SAICA).[4]

A good practice example of collaboration from across a number of accounting organizations is chapter 7: Constructing a Foundational Body of Knowledge (Initial Step: Assembling Accounting Competencies) of The Pathways Commission: Charting a National Strategy for the Next Generation of Accountants.[5] This document offers a good range of non-technical, enabling competencies, as well as lists of technical topic areas. (Note that the document refers to these as "competencies," but using the terminology in this Guide, the technical areas would be more akin to "knowledge topic" listings).

Review Competency Frameworks from other organizations locally, and look for opportunities to collaborate. When researching other relevant competency frameworks, don't overlook other organizations in your own region (including PAOs and, conceivably, universities). Often, even if these aren't as advanced as some of the "best practice" organizations, regional bodies will provide insight into local norms and idiosyncrasies. They may also give examples of condensed approaches that are effective in achieving successes with fewer resources.

Collaborating with other local organizations on national/regional CBAETC initiatives encourages stakeholders to work together in developing key competencies and mutual recognition of qualifications awarded by different accounting education providers. This can result in a more efficient allocation and use of locally-available resources to achieve synergies.

A3. Collect targeted stakeholder input
Identify a core, trusted stakeholder advisory group (task force). Once you have completed your research and reviewed other competency framework examples, you should have some good ideas of the approach you want to use to draft a competency framework and the key reference sources you will rely on. At this point, targeted stakeholder interviews and/or focus groups can further develop your understanding of the competencies appropriate to the environment in

which local professional accountants work. The goal is to get insight from a small, but representative advisory group of respected individuals that can contribute a broad range of perspectives. The groups targeted depend on jurisdiction-specific attributes, but should include:

- Regulators
- Employers, including both larger organizations and small and medium-sized enterprises
- Clients
- Both recently certified and experienced professional accountants
- Experienced accounting educators
- Professional recruiters.

Collect and document input from your advisory group. To gather input, discuss with stakeholders their expectations of what professional accountants should be able to do in a variety of roles, situations and contexts. Distinguish between expectations for newly-qualified members and for experienced members.

A4. Develop preliminary drafts of the required domains, competency statements, and knowledge topics

In drafting a Competency Framework, a PAO need not 'reinvent the wheel'. Your earlier research included examples from PAOs that have already developed comprehensive competency frameworks, some of which build on the earlier work of others. However, the work of others should not be followed blindly because jurisdiction-specific issues (for example, differences in stages of economic development, legal systems, openness of the market, dominant industries, etc.) warrant special consideration. There are also deeper benefits to be gained by developing a unique Competency Framework locally, rather than simply implementing another PAO's Framework directly, such as:

- Deeper understanding of the Framework and how it will be connected to the various aspects of the profession's ambit
- Enhanced stakeholder buy-in for the final Competency Framework
- Greater interaction between the PAO and its stakeholders throughout the process, which strengthens the PAO's network of expertise
- More advanced gap analysis, as different models and statements need to be specifically discussed and debated before inclusion; and
- More effective member communication around the utility of the Framework for both IPD and CPD applications.

Draft the required competency domains. **Competency domains** aim to group the technical and enabling competencies into 10–20 logical groupings that cover the full range of competencies expected of professional accountants.

As an example, CPA Canada specifies the following competency domains:

Technical competency areas
- Financial reporting
- Strategy and governance
- Management accounting
- Audit and assurance
- Finance
- Taxation.

Enabling competency areas
- Professional and ethical behavior
- Problem-solving and decision-making
- Communication
- Self-management
- Teamwork and leadership.

Although technical competencies and enabling competencies are often presented separately in a Competency Framework, as they are in the CPA Canada domains, professional competence requires effective and simultaneous application of both technical and enabling competencies to perform complex tasks at, or above, specified proficiency levels. This means that when you get to the stage where you are designing program elements, you'll ensure that technical and non-technical areas are integrated at the appropriate level.

In addition, it is important to be mindful of the underlying foundational areas that span the competency domains and ensure that these are adequately reflected when competency statements are being drafted. Areas such as business law, economic theory, quantitative methods, and information technology will often not be classified as domains in their own right, but will span other domains. IT, for example, could be reflected in the following competency domains:

- Accounting, with respect to systems and controls
- Auditing, with respect to paperless offices or data analytics
- Finance, with respect to cryptocurrencies and financing models
- Communications, with respect to email etiquette and business use of text messaging.

It is important that these foundational areas be adequately reflected to the extent that they support the roles and expected tasks of professional accountants in your jurisdiction.

See appendix B for a comparison of sample competency domains.

Draft the specific competency statements. Each competency domain houses a number of **competency statements** that describe the knowledge, skills, and attributes expected of members of the profession.

CPA Canada, for example, specifies 17 competency statements that make up the "Financial Reporting" domain, divided into 4 sub-areas, as shown in box 3.1.

Each domain within your Competency Framework should be adequately reflected by your series of competency statements that are consistently structured and presented. As illustrated in CPA Canada's list, each statement should:

- Begin with an appropriate action word that conveys the expected proficiency level
- Be concise; and
- Be consistently structured.

When drafting your competency statements (and when refining them in later steps) it is useful to keep notes on how the statements should be interpreted. For example, CPA Canada describes each of its competencies in terms of a

Financial reporting

Financial reporting needs and systems

1.1.1. Evaluates financial reporting needs

1.1.2. Evaluates the appropriateness of the basis of financial reporting

1.1.3. Evaluates reporting processes to support reliable financial reporting

1.1.4. Explains implications of current trends and emerging issues in financial reporting

1.1.5. Identifies financial reporting needs for the public sector

1.1.6. Identifies specialized financial reporting requirements for specified regulatory and other filing requirements.

Accounting policies and transactions

1.2.1. Develops or evaluates appropriate accounting policies and procedures

1.2.2. Evaluates treatment for routine transactions

1.2.3. Evaluates treatment for non-routine transactions

1.2.4. Analyzes treatment for complex events or transactions.

Financial report preparation

1.3.1. Prepares financial statements

1.3.2. Prepares routine financial statement note disclosure.

Financial statement analysis

1.4.1. Analyzes complex financial statement note disclosure

1.4.2. Evaluates financial statements including note disclosures

1.4.3. Analyzes and provides input in the preparation of the management communication (e.g., management discussion and analysis (MD&A))

1.4.4. Interprets financial reporting results for stakeholders (external or internal)

1.4.5. Analyzes and predicts the impact of strategic and operational decisions on financial results.

Source: CPA Canada.

---

number of outcomes. An example of the outcomes for a sample competency from the Financial Reporting domain is given below (also see box 3.2):

Competency 1.4.4 Interprets financial reporting results for stakeholders (external or internal)

Outcomes:

(1) Prepares and interprets financial statement analysis (e.g., ratios and trend analysis) to support decision-making

(2) Analyzes, interprets, and explains financial statement information to, or for, stakeholders

Draft the lists of knowledge topics. As part of the process, Knowledge Topic Lists are generated for the technical competency statements, to describe the intended scope and context of the statements. Knowledge topics are usually not generated for enabling competencies because enabling competencies are focused on broader behaviors and attitudes, rather than being tied to underlying knowledge, and apply to all contexts.

Knowledge topics may be specified for each technical competency, or they may be developed based on the set of competencies in a technical domain. For example, CPA Canada's knowledge topics are presented based on subtopics that make up the competency domain, and are then mapped to the specific

A practical note on competency statements

When drafting competency statements, it is important to achieve an appropriate level of "granularity."

Competency statements need to be granular enough so that they can be distinguished in terms of mapping and setting proficiency levels. At the same time, however, too much granularity can result in too many statements, such that managing the Framework becomes overly cumbersome. There is no "magic number" as to how many competency statements should make up a Framework, but good practice suggests that somewhere between 125 and 175 statements is an effective choice.

Compare, for example, the following three sample draft competency statements:

(1) Prepares journal entries.

(2) Prepares journal entries in accordance with **IFRS® Standards** for transactions of low to moderate complexity.

(3) Prepares journal entries in accordance with **IFRS® Standards** for sales transactions of large corporations.

Sample 1 is not granular enough for most organizations, as the proficiency level expected will differ between lower- and higher-complexity transactions (so it would be difficult to assign a single proficiency level to the statement). At the other end, developing statements as granular as sample 3 would result in such a long list of statements that the Competency Framework would be unwieldly. Sample 2 offers better balance between the two extremes.

TABLE 3.2 **Sample knowledge topics**

TOPICS	RELATED CPA COMPETENCIES
Introduction to Accounting Objectives and fundamental accounting concepts and principles (qualitative characteristics of accounting information, basic elements)	1.1.1 Evaluates financial reporting needs
	1.1.2 Evaluates the appropriateness of the basis of financial reporting
Ethical professional judgement	1.1.3 Evaluates reporting processes to support reliable financial reporting
Objectives of financial reporting	
Methods of measurement	1.2.1 Develops or evaluates appropriate accounting policies and procedures
Difference between accrual accounting compared to cash accounting	
Framework of standard setting (IFRS and ASPE)	1.4.2 evaluates financial statements including note disclosures
Financial statement users and their broad needs, standard setting, and requirement for accountability	1.4.4 Interprets financial reporting results for stakeholders (external or internal)
Accounting information systems The role of IT in the reporting of information, including: real-time access, remote access to information, dashboard, spreadsheet, report generator, and XBRL (eXtensible Business Reporting Language)	
Emerging trends in accounting standards and recent updates	1.1.4 Explains implications of current trends and emerging issues in financial reporting
Legislation that has an impact on accounting (Sox, Bill 198)	1.1.6 Identifies specialized financial reporting requirements for specified regulatory and other filing requirements

Source: CPA Canada.

competency statements to ensure consistency and alignment. The CPA Canada Knowledge Supplement, which contains the knowledge topic lists, can be found at https://www.cpacanada.ca/en/become-a-cpa/pathways-to-becoming-a-cpa/national-education-resources/the-cpa-competency-map (scroll down to the link to the Knowledge Supplement). A sample of knowledge topics from the Financial Reporting domain is shown in table 3.2.

In the CPA Topic listing, notice the inclusion of foundational areas such as law and IT. This ensures that the full context of the technical competencies is understood.

Knowledge Topics may be assigned their own proficiency levels, or the proficiency levels may be specified only at the level of the competency statements, depending on the PAO.

In some jurisdictions, knowledge topics are mandated through legislation, such as when government ministries set a required list of topics to be taught and examined for licensed auditors. In these cases, the mandated list should be seen as necessary topics for coverage, but it should not be assumed that they are the only topic areas necessary.

There may also be common core curricula that have been developed for a region or group of organizations. A group of European PAOs have collaborated on the Common Content Project, to develop a set of Learning Outcomes, Knowledge requirements and a Skills Framework. Common Content Project resources are available at www.commoncontent.com. Within the set of resources:

> *Learning Outcomes* are statements that are more granular than what would typically be expected of Competency Statements. These are most useful as guidance when developing specific course and professional program elements, as will be discussed in Stage 3.

> *Knowledge requirements* list specific knowledge topics that support the Learning Outcomes. These serve as a valuable reference tool when drafting knowledge topics. They also include "knowledge levels" similar to proficiency levels.

The Skills Framework lists Capability Statements that are written at the level of Competency Statements for enabling competencies.

Once you have drafted a complete set of competency statements to cover the technical and non-technical domains, and have drafted a set of knowledge topics, broad-based consultation is needed to refine the draft into a usable and valid Framework.

B. Broad-based consultation (Practice Analysis)

Broad-based consultation of this type is typically referred to as a **Practice Analysis**. Consultation relies on the expert opinion of experienced professional accountants and other subject-matter experts such as employers, academics, and regulators, that represent the range of contexts, roles and perspectives involved with the profession.

A Practice Analysis is conducted to:

- Validate the chosen competency domains
- Review, validate, and revise (as necessary) the initial working draft of the competency statements
- Ensure that the full range of competencies essential for professional accountants is reflected in the Framework and supported by the knowledge topic list
- Establish required proficiency levels for professional accountants, including any specialities
- Ensure that the proficiency levels established reflect the local context and are realistic based on the local environment
- Generate and encourage buy-in from the broad range of stakeholders who will rely on and use the Competency Framework for future implementation of education, training, and experience assessment programs.

The Practice Analysis should be initiated by the same team that compiled the draft list of competency statements. Performing a Practice Analysis requires extensive expertise and is usually done in conjunction with an independent expert and a psychometrician, to bring specialized expertise, ensure objectivity and avoid potential bias when performing the steps below.

B1. Design and prepare for the Practice Analysis
Create the analysis tools and instruments and develop the methodology. A Practice Analysis usually takes the form of a comprehensive survey, augmented with stakeholder focus groups, where stakeholders identify their competence expectations of newly-certified professional accountants.

Different surveys can be used to capture different perspectives (such as employer versus professional accountant) and to limit the time commitment for each participant. The set of surveys should be designed to produce information about:

- The extent to which the competencies are performed in practice, and whether competency statements may be missing
- The extent to which the knowledge topics are applied in practice, support the competencies, and whether knowledge topics may be missing
- Which competencies are most important to protecting the public and/or responding to the needs of clients and employers
- Which competencies are considered essential to becoming a newly-certified professional accountant
- When a competency or knowledge of a topic should be acquired (before or after certification)
- How a competency is best developed and assessed (through education, exams and/or practical experience)
- The proficiency level required for each competency (and, ideally, knowledge topic) (box 3.3).

If working with an expert/psychometrician, they will have standardized tools and methodologies that can be used efficiently. You should consider testing the surveys on a small pilot group first, to ensure they are clearly worded for respondents.

It is important to remind respondents that their responses should reflect expectations for a *new* member, not a seasoned professional—in other words, they should reflect the *minimum* acceptable level needed to achieve certification.

Determine survey samples and secure sufficient and appropriate participants for focus groups. Participants should include representatives of the same stakeholder groups referred to above with respect to the initial consultation, namely:

- Regulators
- Employers, including larger organizations and small and medium-sized enterprises
- Clients
- Recently certified and experienced professional accountants

BOX 3.3

A practical note on proficiency levels

Many PAOs use numbered or lettered proficiency levels (such as A, B, C or 1, 2, 3). If this approach is used, a decision must be made whether to use 1 (or A) as the highest level or lowest level in the certification program. It is quite common to use 1 (or A) as the highest level, and 3 (or C) as the lowest level. The challenge with this decision, however, is that it limits the ability to denote a higher level expected for experienced members or specialists. For this reason, it may be preferable to use 1 (or A) as the lowest level, so that levels 4 (or D) and beyond remain available for post-certification expectations.

- Experienced accounting educators
- Professional recruiters.

When sampling from the membership, your sampling methodology needs to ensure that the sample will be sufficiently large and diverse to be representative of the profession as a whole. Consider, for example, geographic representation, industry mix, experience levels, and so on. For focus groups, the groups should also be large enough to ensure sufficient breadth and depth of perspective and expertise (including expertise in foundational areas such as business law, economics, quantitative methods, IT, and so on) while balancing the ability to more meaningfully engage with a smaller number of professionals.

For example, an effective approach in holding focus groups is to divide participants into working groups according to their primary competency domains of expertise, and ensure that each domain has sufficient breadth of perspectives within the group. Grouping participants in this way requires advance information on their main competency domains and their backgrounds.

Attend to required logistics and administration. Prepare packages of surveys with clear instructions, using either paper or electronic means depending on the norms of the local context.

With respect to focus groups, the venue chosen should allow for privacy and be set up to facilitate break-out groups and other smaller group discussions. The organization will need to have sufficient, knowledgeable staff on hand to act as an information recorder for each group, to ensure the insights from all participants are clearly and systematically documented. A consistent approach to documenting discussions should be agreed upon prior to hosting the focus groups.

B2. Validate and test the preliminary drafts and set proficiency levels

Administer the surveys. Set a realistic deadline for response, and consider sending reminder messages and using incentives for participating. The higher the response rate, the more reliable the data set to analyze.

Compile the results of the surveys and set proficiency levels. Analyze responses to determine what has been clearly validated or rejected, and use the proficiency level ratings to set proficiency levels for the competency statements and, potentially, knowledge topics. These classifications should be consistent with respondents' rankings of importance and essentiality.

Determine the questions that need to be resolved based on the survey responses. Survey results will likely include some conflicting opinions and ideas, or lack clarity in some areas. These contradictory or unclear results should be systematically noted to be resolved with the focus groups.

Facilitate focus groups. Focus groups allow for more in-depth discussion in specific areas, to resolve the questions that arise from the survey responses and make recommendations on borderline decisions. Strong facilitation skills are needed to ensure that issues are resolved using the groups' expertise as efficiently and effectively as possible.

Compile the results of the focus group discussions. Careful recording of the outcomes of the group discussions is needed to ensure that the information will be clear and easy to interpret when finalizing the Competency Framework, and to maintain appropriate documentation of the process followed.

FIGURE 3.2
Competency Framework structure

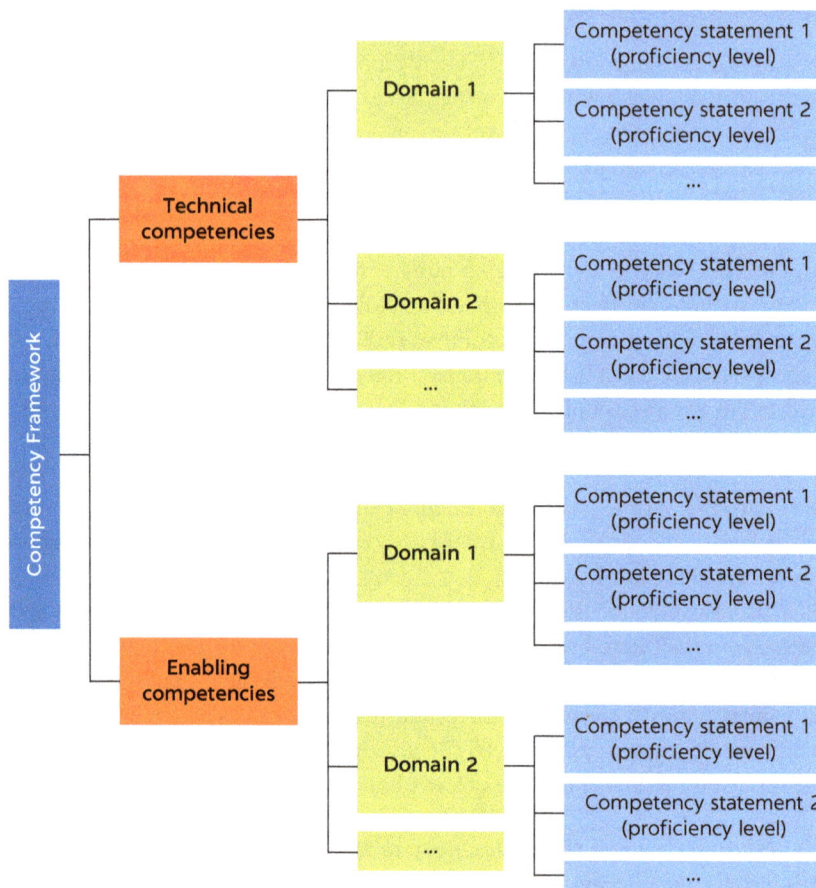

Knowledge Topic Lists are typically compiled in a separate document, referenced back to the Competency Framework.

Results from the Practice Analysis are compiled to allow the draft competency statements, proficiency levels, and related knowledge topics to be finalized in the next step.

C. Initial competency framework

The Practice Analysis will result in a significant amount of input and feedback that must be thoroughly addressed to develop the finalized initial Competency Framework (figure 3.2).

C1. Refine competency statements and proficiency levels
Use the compiled results of the Practice Analysis to refine the draft competency statements. Refinements may include wording changes, combining statements that are seen to be too overlapping, or splitting apart statements that are thought to be too complex or broad.

Use the compiled results of the Practice Analysis to refine the draft proficiency levels. When refining the proficiency levels, you'll need to resolve differences of opinion between participants. During the focus groups and when finalizing the Framework, remember to refer back to the IESs that set minimum proficiency levels for a range of Learning Outcomes. Your own proficiency levels will need to adhere to these requirements. Remember also to ensure that the action word(s) at the beginning of each competency statement correctly captures the expected proficiency level.

Use the compiled results of the Practice Analysis to finalize knowledge topics for each competency that are consistent with the identified proficiency level. Knowledge topics must logically underlie (i.e., be necessary to support) the competency statement(s) they relate to. The various topic lists should be reviewed specifically to ensure that they collectively provide sufficient breadth and scope for the full range of competency statements.

C2. Test the proposed Competency Framework

The final step in developing the Competency Framework is to test the final draft version of the proposed Framework with a limited, but reasonably diverse, group of key stakeholders. The intent at this point is to simply resolve any concerns around confusing wording; conduct a final, reasonableness check as to the completeness of statements and knowledge topics, and appropriateness of proficiency levels; and to ensure that the overall competency profile of a professional accountant is realistic.

Remember that ensuring the requirements are reflective of expectations for a newly-certified individual are the focus for the broader Competency Framework. If your process also included delineating minimum expectations for specialties, such as auditors, these should now be tested with narrower groups of stakeholders more representative of those specialties as well.

C3. Finalize and disseminate the initial Competency Framework

On the basis of any additional feedback received in step C2, and in the context of all earlier research and development, revise, finalize, and distribute the Competency Framework.

Make any necessary final changes to Framework. Any changes to the wording of competencies, knowledge topics, or proficiency levels at this stage should be very carefully considered and limited to "fatal flaw" issues given the extent of input received throughout the preceding process and the importance of maintaining a valid connection to the psychometric aspects of the process.

Widely disseminate the Framework and communicate with all stakeholders. The Framework should be made available to all stakeholders, especially those most involved in the process. As in any change management situation, this distribution should be accompanied by clear communication underscoring the central nature and importance of the Framework, and summarizing the process undertaken, stakeholder groups involved, and the planned next steps.

Milestones of success

You have now developed a fully-validated Competency Framework that your organization and its key stakeholders are confident in, which includes:

- A number of competency domains to provide structure to the Framework
- A complete set of competency statements that encompasses the role of the professional accountant, including any specialties, in your jurisdiction

- Designated proficiency levels for each statement (and, ideally, knowledge topic), based on the role
- Sets of knowledge topics to support each competency domain or statement.

This Competency Framework will serve as the standard against which you map and evaluate your current program elements in Stage 2.

A condensed approach to stage 1: Developing a competency framework

One of the significant challenges of undertaking a full Practice Analysis is that despite its value and importance, it is relatively costly and time consuming. In addition, the Practice Analysis should ideally be undertaken before the accounting education program is developed or in advance of a major program revision, to avoid having to considerably retrofit a program to the Framework. If, however, resources are not available to undertake a full Practice Analysis in the short-term, the following condensed and iterative approach may be considered as a starting point:

- Draw on the experience of established Frameworks and IAESB's IESs
- Draft a set of competency statements and related proficiency levels, as well as the underlying knowledge topics (or descriptions)
- Use a small, but still representative, group of stakeholders to evaluate the Framework in an intensive workshop
- Map the extant pre- and post-certification programs against the Framework, adjusting the programs as needed
- Review and adjust the Framework over time as appropriate, with the goal of completed a full Practice Analysis when resources permit.

Refer to appendix A for a more detailed illustration of using this condensed approach to develop a Competency Framework in Poland.

Additional condensed approach example of creating a common syllabus that moves towards CBAETC

The World Bank's Center for Financial Reporting Reform (CFRR) led a project through its STAREP program (Strengthening Auditing and Reporting in the Countries of the Eastern Partnership) to develop a regional "Common Core Syllabus," which sets out the main capabilities to be obtained by students completing a related undergraduate degree. The syllabus is available in English and Russian, at: www.worldbank.org/cfrr.

The Common Core Syllabus lists Learning Objectives/Main Capabilities, which generally reflect the granularity of competency statements, but are aimed at the university rather than professional level, and do not specify proficiency levels. In this way, the document provides a useful hybrid that can be used:

- By universities, to harmonize accounting curricula in the region, and as a basis of collaboration and mutual exchange
- By PAOs when collaborating with universities and other PAOs to develop and/or recognize courses and program elements (to harmonize programs and avoid duplication)
- By PAOs looking to develop their own Competency Framework (the current list of Learning Objectives/Main Capabilities could be expanded to the professional level and assigned proficiency levels)
- As a resource for other organizations looking to implement CBAETC.

Similarly, a project was led through the PULSAR program (Public Sector Accounting and Reporting) to develop an "Accrual Based Accounting Core Competency Framework for Public Sector Finance Professionals," which links education and training activities to workplace requirements. The Core Competency Framework is available on the PULSAR website in English, Russian, and Bosnian/Serbian/Croatian.[6]

The Core Competency Framework is meant to be used as a guide in defining core competencies with respect to accrual-based accounting for various functional job categories within government, and as such may be modified to adapt to specific needs. In this way, it may be used to support governments in implementing and sustaining reforms toward the adoption of accrual-based accounting.

The Framework identifies:

1. Key functional job categories for which to target training specific to accrual-based accounting reforms
2. Core competencies required for each group to effectively implement and sustain the reforms
3. Suggested proficiency levels for each core competency and functional category, and
4. Associated learning objectives linked with capabilities that demonstrate competence.

A note for trainers of technicians

If your organization trains accounting technicians, it is unlikely that you would go through the full effort and expense of performing a Practice Analysis. To develop a Competency Framework relevant to technicians, you would likely follow a condensed approach, reviewing established Competency Frameworks in your region and selecting the subset of foundational competencies to be developed at the technician level. You could then set proficiency levels that are applicable for your students, based on the roles they are being developed to take on in the market.

This can be particularly beneficial if the PAO in your jurisdiction has an established Competency Framework. If so, mapping your program's learning outcomes and proficiency levels to the PAO's Framework can serve as a starting point for collaborating on an agreed-upon understanding of the advance standing that could be offered to technicians who wish to bridge into the PAO's professional program.

If there is no Competency Framework to draw on, you may decide to define the program content in terms of tasks and roles expected to be performed by those who complete the program. For an example of this approach, see appendix A6.

STAGE 2: EVALUATE THE CURRENT PROGRAM TO DETERMINE GAPS

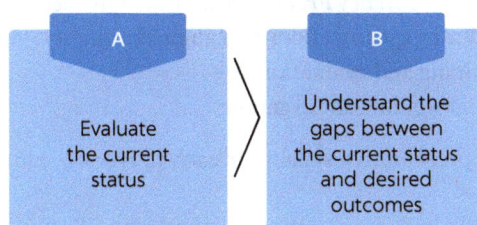

A — Evaluate the current status

B — Understand the gaps between the current status and desired outcomes

This stage requires a systematic and thorough assessment of the extent of competence that is developed by current program requirements.

There are two facets to this stage:

1. Evaluating the competence level expected to be achieved through IPD program requirements (education, exams/evaluations, and experience) that a potential candidate needs to successfully demonstrate before being granted certification as a professional accountant; and
2. Evaluating the level of competence maintained by experienced members. This second element is necessary because if there are gaps in the competence level attained through IPD, it is important to understand to what degree these gaps still exist for experienced members, and to what extent they have been filled through ongoing experience and/or CPD.

These facets will be described sequentially below, but can be performed in parallel.

Note that if your Competency Framework includes different competencies and/or proficiency levels for specializations such as audit, you will need to evaluate the current program requirements to become authorized to perform the specialty (such as achieving an audit license) against the required competencies and proficiency levels in the Competency Framework. You would also want to consider assessing the competence of current practicing auditors.

A. Evaluate the current status

A1. In consultation with key stakeholders, review the current certification program elements

Prepare a comprehensive inventory of the **program elements.** Prepare a list of education, evaluations, and practical experience elements.

For example, assume your IPD program requires candidates to:

- Complete an undergraduate economics degree, including specified courses, at a state-accredited university
- Pass a series of licensing exams set by the PAO
- Complete 3 years of work experience under the supervision of a licensed accountant, and
- Swear an oath to abide by the PAO's bylaws and code of conduct.

In your inventory, you would list:

- Each mandatory and elective course typically included in an accredited degree program
- Each course and exam required to be completed through the PAO
- The PAO's work experience requirements, and
- Any guidance or additional instruction given to candidates before they swear the oath.

For each element, obtain and review the detail available to support mapping the element to the Competency Framework. The detail needed to support mapping would include any specifications that guide the quality, depth, and breadth of instruction, training and evaluation.

For example, you would want to gather:

- Standard or representative syllabi for each university course that must be completed
- Course materials, including textbooks and other readings

- Expected learning outcomes provided in syllabi and/or textbooks
- Sample exams from university courses (including sample marking keys or rubrics)
- Sample professional certification exams
- Design documents or blueprints for courses and exams
- Requirements for work experience that go beyond time requirements (such as requirements for progressive levels of responsibility, expectations that need to be met through performance evaluations, breadth requirements, etc.).

A2. Map the current elements to the framework

For each element, cross reference the components to the Competency Framework.
Each element of the program will have a number of **components**. For example, each course will be comprised of lessons or modules supported by textbooks or other materials. Professional exams may be broken into sections covering different subjects or topics, and there may be professional courses that precede each exam. A training program may also have parts or sets of requirements (such as requiring a certain number of hours of audit or tax work to be included). The question you want to answer for each of these components is "What competency (or competencies) is (are) supported by this component, and to what proficiency level?"

Your mapping needs to cross reference program elements to both the technical and enabling competencies. From a practical perspective, it may be easier to separate the technical mapping from the mapping of enabling skills.

Mapping to technical competencies

Assuming that in Stage 1 you developed a full set of knowledge topics mapped to your technical competencies, the most intuitive way to cross-reference course materials and exam components to the technical competencies is usually at the level of knowledge topics. (This can also highlight gaps better than mapping to competencies directly, which will be helpful in step B of this stage). When mapping courses and related evaluations, you'll need to consider the content of the materials, including, for example, the learning objectives provided in the course syllabus and/or textbook, as well exam blueprints, sample exams and marking rubrics, projects and assignments, and so on.

As an illustration of the process, assume that your Competency Framework includes the competency indicated in table 3.3 within the Financial Accounting and Reporting domain, supported by the knowledge topics listed. Note that the competency and the knowledge topics have each been assigned proficiency levels (which happen to all be "Advanced" for these fundamental topics).

Assume also that your organization's program for becoming certified as a professional accountant includes the following elements that support Financial Accounting and Reporting competencies:

- Two financial accounting courses taken as part of an undergraduate degree
- A licensing exam set by the PAO, and
- 3 years of experience under the supervision of a licensed member of the profession.

To map each of the courses to this technical competency:

1. Gather the syllabus, textbook, other readings and materials, as well as samples of the assignments and exams (with solutions) for each course
2. Use the syllabus, textbook, other readings and materials to determine and document the knowledge topics covered in the courses

TABLE 3.3 **Competency domain: Financial accounting and reporting**

FAR-4 Evaluates routine transactions to determine the appropriate accounting treatment

Required Proficiency Level | Advanced

Description: evaluates source documents and information about routine events and transactions, and determines the appropriate accounting treatment; records routine transactions accurately

KNOWLEDGE TOPIC	PROFICIENCY LEVELS[a] FRAMEWORK
Accounting for:	
• Cash and cash equivalents	A
• Receivables	A
• Inventories	A
• Property, plant, and equipment	A
• Goodwill and intangible assets	A
• Depreciation and amortization	A
• Impairment, and disposition/derecognition	A
• Payables	A
• Provisions and contingencies	A
• Long-term liabilities	A
• Owners'/shareholders' equity	A
• Earnings per share (basic, diluted)	A
• Financial instruments	A
• Investments in associates/significant influence	A
• Revenue recognition/revenue from contracts with customers, and accounting for revenue and related expenses	A
• Leases	A
• Changes in accounting policies and estimates, and errors	A
• Foreign currency transactions	A
• Accounting for income taxes	A
• Events after the reporting period	A

a. Proficiency levels: A = Advanced I = Intermediate F = Foundation.

3. Review the assignments, exams, and other evaluations in the courses to see what cognitive level is being assessed (based on Bloom's Taxonomy (Anderson et al. 2001) or a similar scheme)
4. Estimate the proficiency level of each knowledge topic supported by the course requirements.

When estimating proficiency levels:

- Consider the depth, breadth, cognitive level and amount of coverage of each knowledge topic
- Pay attention to the instructional methodology used, and the expectations placed on candidates while completing the components
- Recall that requiring candidates to memorize and recite information will only support a low level of proficiency, whereas testing candidates on their ability to integrate, apply concepts and make judgments supports an advanced level of proficiency
- Base your evaluation on what level of proficiency is both developed *and tested*. For instance, if candidate performance is evaluated at an intermediate level, it would be incorrect to say that competence is supported at an advanced level.

Your mapping of the two courses may end up looking something like table 3.4.

TABLE 3.4 **Sample mapping**

KNOWLEDGE TOPIC	PROFICIENCY LEVELS[a]		
	FRAMEWORK	COURSE 1	COURSE 2
Accounting for:			
• Cash and cash equivalents	A	F	I
• Receivables	A	F	I
• Inventories	A	F	I
• Property, plant, and equipment	A	F	I
• Goodwill and intangible assets	A		I
• Depreciation and amortization	A	F	I
• Impairment, and disposition/derecognition	A		F
• Payables	A	F	I
• Provisions and contingencies	A		
• Long-term liabilities	A	F	I
• Owners'/shareholders' equity	A	F	I
• Earnings per share (basic, diluted)	A	F	I
• Financial instruments	A		I
• Investments in associates/significant influence	A		F
• Revenue recognition/revenue from contracts with customers, and accounting for revenue and related expenses	A	F	I
• Leases	A	F	I
• Changes in accounting policies and estimates, and errors	A		F
• Foreign currency transactions	A		F
• Accounting for income taxes	A	F	I
• Events after the reporting period	A		F

a. Proficiency levels: A = Advanced I = Intermediate F = Foundation.

This type of mapping becomes challenging when not all elements are standardized. For example, if your program has a degree requirement, but candidates are allowed to complete their degree at any university and the required courses differ significantly between universities, it is difficult to determine what is "typical."

Next, map the PAO exam to the Framework, by cross-referencing the examinable topics listed in the **examination blueprint** to the required knowledge topics. If your organization does not yet have an exam blueprint, you will need to consider which topics are currently examinable, perhaps using several past exams as a reference source. Consider the cognitive level required to succeed on the exam (as evidenced in the past and/or sample exam solutions/rubric) when determining each proficiency level being supported.

Add this information to your course mapping (table 3.5).

Finally, map the experience requirement. To do this, you'll need to consider the specific guidance given to candidates with respect to experience requirements (such as breadth and depth of tasks that need to be performed, minimum hours required in certain tasks or roles, and so on). If there are no mandatory requirements on certain tasks or roles, your estimate of proficiency levels will be informed by the set of tasks that can reasonably be expected to be completed by *all* candidates based on the current program.

Adding in your assessment of work experience may result in a map that looks like this table 3.6.

TABLE 3.5 **Sample mapping plus PAO exam cross-referencing**

KNOWLEDGE TOPIC	PROFICIENCY LEVELS[a]			
	FRAMEWORK	COURSE 1	COURSE 2	PAO EXAM
Accounting for:				
• Cash and cash equivalents	A	F	I	A
• Receivables	A	F	I	A
• Inventories	A	F	I	A
• Property, plant, and equipment	A	F	I	I
• Goodwill and intangible assets	A		I	I
• Depreciation and amortization	A	F	I	A
• Impairment, and disposition/derecognition	A		F	F
• Payables	A	F	I	A
• Provisions and contingencies	A			
• Long-term liabilities	A	F	I	I
• Owners'/shareholders' equity	A	F	I	I
• Earnings per share (basic, diluted)	A	F	I	I
• Financial instruments	A		I	I
• Investments in associates/significant influence	A		F	F
• Revenue recognition/revenue from contracts with customers, and accounting for revenue and related expenses	A	F	I	A
• Leases	A	F	I	I
• Changes in accounting policies and estimates, and errors	A		F	I
• Foreign currency transactions	A		F	I
• Accounting for income taxes	A	F	I	A
• Events after the reporting period	A		F	I

a. Proficiency Levels: A = Advanced I = Intermediate F = Foundation.

TABLE 3.6 **Sample mapping plus work experience assessment**

KNOWLEDGE TOPIC	PROFICIENCY LEVELS[a]				
	FRAMEWORK	COURSE 1	COURSE 2	PAO EXAM	EXPERIENCE
Accounting for:					
• Cash and cash equivalents	A	F	I	A	A
• Receivables	A	F	I	A	A
• Inventories	A	F	I	A	A
• Property, plant, and equipment	A	F	I	I	I
• Goodwill and intangible assets	A		I	I	F
• Depreciation and amortization	A	F	I	A	A
• Impairment, and disposition/derecognition	A		F	F	F
• Payables	A	F	I	A	A
• Provisions and contingencies	A				
• Long-term liabilities	A	F	I	I	A
• Owners'/shareholders' equity	A	F	I	I	I
• Earnings per share (basic, diluted)	A	F	I	I	I
• Financial instruments	A		I	I	I
• Investments in associates/significant influence	A		F	F	F
• Revenue recognition/revenue from contracts with customers, and accounting for revenue and related expenses	A	F	I	A	A
• Leases	A	F	I	I	I
• Changes in accounting policies and estimates, and errors	A		F	I	F
• Foreign currency transactions	A		F	I	A
• Accounting for income taxes	A	F	I	A	A
• Events after the reporting period	A		F	I	F

a. Proficiency levels: A = Advanced I = Intermediate F = Foundation.

Once all related elements have been mapped, you can assign what the overall proficiency levels are deemed to be for the current program's Knowledge Topics. There is some judgment required in making the determination of the current overall proficiency level based on a holistic consideration of coverage through each element. For example, even though the Knowledge Topic "Foreign currency transactions" was evaluated at an "A" proficiency level through practical experience, based on the program overall, comfort was only deemed possible at an "I" level.

The same process is used to map the program elements to each of the technical competencies in the Competency Framework. Note that this example (table 3.7) has shown a single competency being mapped individually, but when actually performing a mapping exercise, elements are usually mapped to all competencies in the relevant domain(s) at the same time to increase efficiency and consistency.

Mapping to enabling competencies

As previously stated, program elements also need to be mapped to the enabling competencies. This requires examining the instructional and assessment methodologies used and the extent to which candidates are required (within education, exams/evaluations, and practical experience) to:

- Think critically
- Apply judgment
- Integrate concepts across domains
- Evaluate situations in the context of professional standards

TABLE 3.7 **Mapping program elements to technical competencies**

KNOWLEDGE TOPIC	PROFICIENCY LEVELS[a]					
	FRAMEWORK	COURSE 1	COURSE 2	PAO EXAM	EXPERIENCE	OVERALL
Accounting for:						
• Cash and cash equivalents	A	F	I	A	A	A
• Receivables	A	F	I	A	A	A
• Inventories	A	F	I	A	A	A
• Property, plant, and equipment	A	F	I	I	I	I
• Goodwill and intangible assets	A		I	I	F	I
• Depreciation and amortization	A	F	I	A	A	A
• Impairment, and disposition/derecognition	A		F	F	F	F
• Payables	A	F	I	A	A	A
• Provisions and contingencies	A					
• Long-term liabilities	A	F	I	I	A	A
• Owners'/shareholders' equity	A	F	I	I	I	I
• Earnings per share (basic, diluted)	A	F	I	I	I	I
• Financial instruments	A		I	I	I	I
• Investments in associates/significant influence	A		F	F	F	F
• Revenue recognition/revenue from contracts with customers, and accounting for revenue and related expenses	A	F	I	A	A	A
• Leases	A	F	I	I	I	I
• Changes in accounting policies and estimates, and errors	A		F	I	F	F
• Foreign currency transactions	A		F	I	A	I
• Accounting for income taxes	A	F	I	A	A	I
• Events after the reporting period	A		F	I	F	F

a. Proficiency levels: A = Advanced I = Intermediate F = Foundation.

- Work as a team and demonstrate leadership
- Communicate professionally to stakeholders, and
- Demonstrate commitment to the public interest.

For example, if a course in the program requires candidates to write realistic business memos, this would support communication competencies. If they are required to critique the work of others, this supports critical thinking, teamwork and leadership. With respect to practical experience requirements, candidates may be expected to take on supervisory tasks as they progress, and workplace mentors may be required to evaluate and confirm a candidate's enabling competencies at various points of their experience.

Carrying on with our mapping illustration, you would map the two financial accounting courses plus all of the other courses in the undergraduate requirement, the licensing exam, and the work experience. For each element, consider questions such as:

- In supporting the communication competencies, to what extent are candidates required to prepare written answers that simulate real business documents (emails, memos, reports, draft policies, working papers, etc.) and to prepare and deliver presentations or complete oral exams?
- How are candidates' communication skills assessed? For example, are specific marks allocated for communication in assignments and on exams?
- Are candidates evaluated on their ability to ensure that their communications are appropriate for their audience?
- In supporting professional and ethical behavior, are ethical dilemmas included in mandatory assignments and exams? If so, how complex, realistic, and integrative are these exercises? Do these exercises tie directly to the current IESBA *International Code of Ethics for Professional Accountants*™ or the local equivalent?
- In the work environment, to what extent do supervisors and mentors formally develop and evaluate candidates' communication with colleagues and clients, and how is feedback for improvement provided to candidates?
- How is ethical behavior and decision-making incorporated within the performance measurement system of the candidates' workplace?
- What obligations are placed on mentors and supervisors to evaluate and report to the PAO with respect to developing candidate competence?

Based on your evaluation of the program elements your mapping to these selected enabling competencies may look like this table 3.8.

Once all of the program elements have been mapped to the full Competency Framework, you're ready to move on to the next step and assess the overall proficiency levels supported for each of the competencies in the Framework.

Assess the proficiency level to which each of the required competencies is covered. Based on the mapping of all components to the Framework, estimate the proficiency level achieved by successful candidates for each Competency Statement. Remember that you are assessing competence, not knowledge. In other words, you're assessing how well a candidate can perform the role and tasks expected of a professional accountant, rather than how well they can recite information from a textbook or tax statute.

Supporting an advanced level of proficiency will require multiple touchpoints. It is highly unlikely for a candidate to gain an advanced level of proficiency through education in a single course alone; rather, exposure through

TABLE 3.8 **Sample mapping of program elements to selected competencies**

| COMPETENCY DOMAIN: COMMUNICATION | PROFICIENCY LEVELS[a] | | | | | | |
	FRAMEWORK	COURSE 1	COURSE 2	COURSE 3	...	PAO EXAM	EXPERIENCE
COM-1 Communicates logically, clearly, and concisely	I	F	I	F	...	I	I
Description: organizes written and spoken communications to present information logically and clearly in as concise a form as possible; provides sufficient rationale for decisions and recommendations							
COM-2 Adapts terminology, information content, and degree of detail for intended user(s)	I		I	F	...	I	I
Description: evaluates the needs and sophistication levels of the intended audience and adjusts the scope, technical level, terminology, and tone to best reflect the audience							
...	...	...	...	...	...	...	...
Competency Domain: Professional and ethical behaviour							
PEB-3 Evaluates situations from an ethics perspective	A		F	F	...	I	I
Description: anticipates and identifies ethics situations as they arise							
PEB-4 Makes decisions in accordance with standards of professional conduct	A		F	F	...	I	I
Description: uses the standards of conduct to determine and support an appropriate course of action							
...	...	...	...	...	...	...	...

a. Proficiency Levels: A = Advanced I = Intermediate F = Foundation.

multiple courses and/or exams should be required, preferably with practical experience rounding out the requirements.

Revisiting our example: After mapping all of the program components, your overall assessment of proficiency levels for the sample competencies might be as shown in tables 3.9 and 3.10.

An example of using a condensed approach to mapping existing program elements to competency requirements is illustrated in appendix A, where the CFRR used a benchmarking study in Serbia to help understand gaps in accounting and audit curricula.

In Step B of this Stage, we'll look at understanding the gaps between the current status and the desired state (as shown in the Framework). Before we perform the gap analysis, however, we also need to estimate the current state of competence for existing professional accountants.

A3. In consultation with key stakeholders, review and document the competence level of current professional accountants

Needless to say, this step can be sensitive as existing professionals are unlikely to want to have their competence directly assessed. The goal should not be individual assessment, but rather reaching an honest conclusion about the profession as a whole and/or its specialties.

TABLE 3.9 **Sample assessment of proficiency levels for financial accounting and reporting**

COMPETENCY DOMAIN: FINANCIAL ACCOUNTING AND REPORTING	PROFICIENCY LEVELS[a]							
	FRAMEWORK	COURSE 1	COURSE 2	COURSE 3	...	PAO EXAM	EXPERIENCE	OVERALL
...	...	...	...	...	...	...	...	...
FAR-4 Evaluates routine transactions to determine the appropriate accounting treatment	A	F	F/I			I/A	I	I
Description: evaluates source documents and information about routine events and transactions, and determines the appropriate accounting treatment; records routine transactions accurately								
...	...	...	...	...	... ...		...	...

a. Proficiency levels: A = Advanced I = Intermediate F = Foundation

TABLE 3.10 **Sample assessment of proficiency levels for communication**

COMPETENCY DOMAIN: COMMUNICATION	PROFICIENCY LEVELS[a]							
	FRAMEWORK	COURSE 1	COURSE 2	COURSE 3	...	PAO EXAM	EXPERIENCE	OVERALL
...	...	...	...	...	...	...	...	...
COM-1 Communicates logically, clearly, and concisely	I	F	I	F	...	I	I	I
Description: organizes written and spoken communications to present information logically and clearly in as concise a form as possible; provides sufficient rationale for decisions and recommendations								
COM-2 Adapts Communications for intended user(s)	I		I	F	...	I	I	I
Description: evaluates the needs and sophistication levels of the intended audience and adjusts the scope, technical level, terminology, and tone to best reflect the audience								
...	...	...	...	...	...	...	...	...
Competency Domain: Professional and ethical behaviour								
...	...	...	...	...	...	...	...	...
PEB-3 Evaluates situations from an ethics perspective	A		F	F	...	I	I	I
Description: anticipates and identifies ethics situations as they arise								
PEB-4 Makes decisions in accordance with standards of professional conduct	A		F	F	...	I	I	I
Description: uses the standards of conduct to determine and support an appropriate course of action								
...	...	...	...	...	...	...	...	...

a. Proficiency levels: A = Advanced I = Intermediate F = Foundation

Review any research conducted on the competence of local professional accountants (such as in a ROSC A&A). This research can help to inform your overall assessment and provide objective background context.

Review recent findings from the compliance and discipline department of the PAO(s). Competence issues may become apparent through analyzing trends in the complaints received regarding members and/or through the results of regulatory inspection and review processes.

For example, practice inspection results can highlight areas where practitioners are collectively weaker and having challenges meeting standards. This may include technical competency domains such as assurance or tax, as well as enabling competencies, such as a lack of ability to apply the Code of Professional Conduct with respect to independence obligations. Complaints from the public can also point to areas where competence should be enhanced.

Use focus groups, surveys and/or interviews to have knowledgeable stakeholders assess the competence of professional accountants across the Framework. Ideally, you want to gain insight from people who oversee the work of professional accountants with real-world experience.

For example, consider including members of your focus groups from your Practice Analysis. You can also ask a representative sample of current members to anonymously self-assess their competence.

Remember that if your Framework required different competencies and/or proficiency levels for specializations such as auditors, you should also assess the competence of these subgroups using the same process.

Compile the results of your evaluations. The easiest way to do this is to use a copy of the Competency Framework and record the estimated current proficiency level for each competency.

As an illustration, your evaluation of competence may result in the following ratings for the sample of competencies shown:

If you are tracking specializations separately, you would compile an evaluation for each specialization being considered (table 3.11).

Once you've completed mapping and determined proficiency levels for the current certification program and for existing professionals practicing in the market, you're ready to move on to performing a systematic gap analysis.

TABLE 3.11 Sample tracking of specializations

COMPETENCY DOMAIN: FINANCIAL ACCOUNTING AND REPORTING	PROFICIENCY LEVELS[a]	
	FRAMEWORK	CURRENT
...	...	...
FAR-4 Evaluates routine transactions to determine the appropriate accounting treatment	A	I
FAR-5 Evaluates complex non-routine transactions to determine the appropriate accounting treatment	I	F
FAR-8 Prepares or evaluates financial statement note disclosure	A	I
...	...	...
Competency Domain: Management accounting		
...	...	...
MA-2 Prepares, analyzes, or evaluates operational plans, budgets, and forecasts	A	I
MA-6 Evaluates root causes of operational performance issues	I	F
...	...	...
COMPETENCY DOMAIN: ASSURANCE		
...	...	...
A-1 Evaluates client acceptance and continuance in the context of independence and other professional standards	A	F
A-7 Explains the implications of pending changes in assurance standards	I	F
...	...	...

continued

TABLE 3.11 continued

COMPETENCY DOMAIN: TAXATION		
...	...	...
TX-1 Determines tax payable in routine situations	I	A
TX-3 Determines tax implications of potential business transactions	I	I
...	...	...
COMPETENCY DOMAIN: COMMUNICATION		
...	...	...
COM-1 Communicates logically, clearly, and concisely	I	A
COM-2 Adapts communications for intended user(s)	I	I
...	...	...
Competency domain: Personal management		
...	...	...
PM-3 Demonstrates a commitment to lifelong learning	A	F
...	...	...
TL-1 Contributes effectively as a member of a team	A	A
TL-2 Manages conflicts between team members	I	I
COMPETENCY DOMAIN: COMMUNICATION		
TL-3 Promotes team diversity and participation	A	I
...	...	...
Competency domain: Professional and ethical behavior		
...	...	...
PEB-3 Evaluates situations from an ethics perspective	A	I
PEB-4 Makes decisions in accordance with standards of professional conduct	A	F
...	...	...

a. Proficiency levels: A = Advanced I = Intermediate F = Foundation

B. Understand the gaps between the current status and the desired outcomes

B1. Determine the extent to which current IPD program elements support the requirements in the Competency Framework and document the gaps

Compare the proficiency levels that were assessed as being currently supported (in step A2 above) against the required proficiency levels. Note: you've already done the background work required for this step. At this point, you are simply systematically comparing the current proficiency ratings against the required "Framework" ratings to determine which competencies are adequately being covered by the current program and which are not.

Returning to the illustration from Step A results in table 3.12.

This comparison should be completed for the program as a whole and can also be done at interim points where appropriate, as well as for any specializations. Wherever you set proficiency levels (i.e., at the end of IPD, at interim points, and/or for licensing under a specialization), perform a gap analysis against that level of proficiency using all of the elements that immediately precede the point where proficiency is expected.

For example, if your Competency Framework sets a proficiency level requirement for entering the professional program as well as at the end of IPD (as illustrated in appendix B), you should perform a gap analysis at both points. If only one proficiency level is set, most commonly at the end of IPD, then your gap analysis will be focused on that point.

TABLE 3.12 **Sample comparison of current proficiency ratings against Framework ratings**

COMPETENCY DOMAIN: FINANCIAL ACCOUNTING AND REPORTING	PROFICIENCY LEVELS[a]							
	FRAMEWORK	COURSE 1	COURSE 2	COURSE 3	...	PAO EXAM	EXPERIENCE	OVERALL
		←		Compare			→	
...	...	...	...	...	...	...	...	...
FAR-4 Evaluates routine transactions to determine the appropriate accounting treatment	A	F	F/I			I/A	I	I
Description: evaluates source documents and information about routine events and transactions, and determines the appropriate accounting treatment; records routine transactions accurately								
COM-1 Communicates logically, clearly, and concisely	I	F	I	F	...	I	I	I
Description: organizes written and spoken communications to present information logically and clearly in as concise a form as possible; provides sufficient rationale for decisions and recommendations								
COM-2 Adapts Communications for intended user(s)	I		I	F	...	I	I	I
Description: evaluates the needs and sophistication levels of the intended audience and adjusts the scope, technical level, terminology, and tone to best reflect the audience								
...	...	...	...	...	...	...	...	...
COMPETENCY DOMAIN: PROFESSIONAL AND ETHICAL BEHAVIOUR								
PEB-3 Evaluates situations from an ethics perspective	A		F	F	...	I	I	I
Description: anticipates and identifies ethics situations as they arise								
PEB-4 Makes decisions in accordance with standards of professional conduct	A		F	F	...	I	I	I
Description: uses the standards of conduct to determine and support an appropriate course of action								

a. Proficiency levels: A = Advanced I = Intermediate F = Foundation

Document what competencies are sufficiently covered by the program elements and which ones have gaps. This assessment is not an exact science, but you are trying to answer questions such as: "By completing the required education and examinations, would a candidate develop and be able to demonstrate competency *X* at the expected proficiency level, or do they reach this level in conjunction with experience, or do they not reach the desired proficiency level at all based on the current requirements?"

This would lead to a gap document that looks similar to the following table 3.13.

The gap document will be heavily relied upon in Stage 3, when designing new program elements.

Lack of standardized requirements pose challenges for assessing competence coverage, as it results in statements such as "If a candidate went to University *A*, they would have been expected to develop this competency, but at University *B*

TABLE 3.13 **Sample gap document**

COMPETENCY DOMAIN: FINANCIAL ACCOUNTING AND REPORTING	PROFICIENCY LEVELS[a]							
	FRAMEWORK	COURSE 1	COURSE 2	COURSE 3	...	PAO EXAM	EXPERIENCE	OVERALL
...	...	...	...	...	...	...	...	...
FAR-4 Evaluates routine transactions to determine the appropriate accounting treatment	A	F	F/I			I/A	I	I
Description: evaluates source documents and information about routine events and transactions, and determines the appropriate accounting treatment; records routine transactions accurately								
COMPETENCY DOMAIN: COMMUNICATION								
COM-1 Communicates logically, clearly, and concisely	I	F	I	F	...	I	I	I
Description: organizes written and spoken communications to present information logically and clearly in as concise a form as possible; provides sufficient rationale for decisions and recommendations								
COM-2 Adapts Communications for intended user(s)	I		I	F	...	I	I	I
Description: evaluates the needs and sophistication levels of the intended audience and adjusts the scope, technical level, terminology, and tone to best reflect the audience								
COMPETENCY DOMAIN: PROFESSIONAL AND ETHICAL BEHAVIOUR								
PEB-3 Evaluates situations from an ethics perspective	A		F	F	...	I	I	I
Description: anticipates and identifies ethics situations as they arise								
PEB-4 Makes decisions in accordance with standards of professional conduct	A		F	F	...	I	I	I
Description: uses the standards of conduct to determine and support an appropriate course of action								

a. Proficiency levels: A = Advanced I = Intermediate F = Foundation.

they may not." Similarly, if the quality of instruction is materially different between universities, the assessment process becomes difficult to track. These variations can, however, be very instructive in the next stage when designing new and enhanced programs (for example, when setting new syllabus requirements for university courses that will be accredited, or for establishing professional programs by a PAO).

B2. Determine and document the gaps between the expected competence level and the current level for professional accountants in practice
Compare and document the required proficiency levels (from the Framework) against the estimated current proficiency levels recorded in step A3 above.

As in Step B1, you've already completed the background work required for this step. At this point, you just need to systematically compare the "current" proficiency ratings against the "Framework" requirements.

Clear documentation will help you design methods to close the gaps in the next stage (table 3.14).

Once again, remember to compile a gap document for any specializations that are being tracked separately.

Now is also an appropriate time to revisit the budget and update it based on what you have learned about the strengths and weaknesses of the current program. The gap analysis performed in this stage will allow you to refine the priorities for implementation, as well as the cost estimates for designing and implementing enhanced program elements.

TABLE 3.14 **Sample comparison of proficiency levels**

COMPETENCY DOMAIN: FINANCIAL ACCOUNTING AND REPORTING	PROFICIENCY LEVELS[a]	
	FRAMEWORK	CURRENT
	← Compare →	
FAR-4 Evaluates routine transactions to determine the appropriate accounting treatment	A	I
FAR-5 Evaluates complex non-routine transactions to determine the appropriate accounting treatment	I	F
FAR-8 Prepares or evaluates financial statement note disclosure	A	I
COMPETENCY DOMAIN: MANAGEMENT ACCOUNTING		
MA-2 Prepares, analyzes, or evaluates operational plans, budgets, and forecasts	A	I
MA-6 Evaluates root causes of operational performance issues	I	F
COMPETENCY DOMAIN: ASSURANCE		
A-1 Evaluates client acceptance and continuance in the context of independence and other professional standards	A	F
A-7 Explains the implications of pending changes in assurance standards	I	F
COMPETENCY DOMAIN: TAXATION		
TX-1 Determines tax payable in routine situations	I	A
TX-3 Determines tax implications of potential business transactions	I	I
COMPETENCY DOMAIN: COMMUNICATION		
COM-1 Communicates logically, clearly, and concisely	I	A
COM-2 Adapts communications for intended user(s)	I	I
COMPETENCY DOMAIN: PERSONAL MANAGEMENT		
PM-3 Demonstrates a commitment to lifelong learning	A	F
COMPETENCY DOMAIN: TEAMWORK AND LEADERSHIP		
TL-1 Contributes effectively as a member of a team	A	A
TL-2 Manages conflicts between team members		
TL-3 Promotes team diversity and participation		
COMPETENCY DOMAIN: PROFESSIONAL AND ETHICAL BEHAVIOR		
PEB-3 Evaluates situations from an ethics perspective	A	I
PEB-4 Makes decisions in accordance with standards of professional conduct	A	I

a. Proficiency Levels: A = Advanced I = Intermediate F = Foundation.

The gap document(s) will be used in Stage 3 when designing enhanced CPD requirements and programs.

Milestones of success

You have now compiled a complete inventory of IPD and CPD program elements mapped to your Competency Framework and evaluated the current programs against the ideals you developed in Stage 1.

At this point in your journey, you have gained a great deal of valuable insight into the current status of accounting education in your jurisdiction, including its strengths and weaknesses.

The mapping documents and gap analyses you created will guide your development of new program elements in Stage 3 (including IPD and CPD).

A CONDENSED APPROACH TO STAGE 2: EVALUATE THE CURRENT PROGRAM TO DETERMINE GAPS

Determining gaps in the IPD program

Viable methods of determining gaps using less resource-intensive methods will depend on the starting point you're working with. If, during Stage 1, you developed a complete Competency Framework (using either the comprehensive or condensed method), and you have developed a list of knowledge topics with proficiency levels, it is well worth the effort to do a full mapping of the current program elements to the Competency Framework. This does not need to be overly resource-intensive, but it is critical that those individuals performing the mapping have a full and realistic understanding of the current program elements and requirements. In other words, that the evaluators can go beyond the syllabus as presented "on paper" and objectively interpret the actual proficiency levels being developed and assessed.

Note: In the case where there are a large number of tertiary education providers that candidates might use to complete the education component, consider beginning the evaluation and mapping process with only a few institutions to ensure the process isn't overwhelmed at the outset. Selecting some of the most advanced institutions first can be more efficient as these will likely be the more administratively organized and also provide the highest current coverage of requirements.

If your Competency Framework does not include full knowledge topics and proficiency levels, you may need to undertake a more high-level anecdotal review, using extremely knowledgeable individuals who can evaluate the program elements holistically against the requirements through the lens of international best practice.

Determining gaps in the competence of existing members

A condensed approach for determining gaps in the competence of existing professional accountants would be to forego evaluating each competency, and instead limit your evaluations to:

- Reviewing any relevant findings and commentary in a recent ROSC A&A
- Reviewing compliance and discipline department findings for current trends, and

- Using interviews with trusted experts to gain perspective on where there may be weaknesses in technical and/or enabling competencies of practicing professional accountants.

If a condensed approach is used, be sure to:

- Include assessment of enabling competencies, as these are just as important (and, in some circumstances, more important) than technical competence
- Consider competence requirements and gaps for specializations as well as for all professional accountants.

STAGE 3: DESIGN AND DEVELOP AN EXPANDED PROGRAM

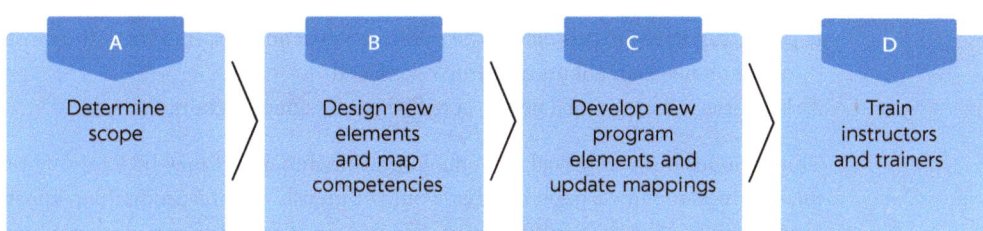

A	B	C	D
Determine scope	Design new elements and map competencies	Develop new program elements and update mappings	Train instructors and trainers

This stage walks through the steps involved in designing and developing new or enhanced program elements based on the results of your gap analysis.

Before embarking on development work, it is important to take the time to design the new or enhanced elements. This ensures that once development work starts, a balanced approach can be taken to developing all necessary elements in parallel (as resources allow), and that prioritization can be adhered to. It is not uncommon to iterate and re-tweak designs once development has begun, as new information comes to light. Nevertheless, having a preliminary design up-front will serve as grounding for ongoing development.

Similarly, it is essential that design activities be undertaken with due consideration of the budget for development and implementation. Throughout the process of designing element enhancements, ensure that you revisit the budget and adjust it as needed based on new information, priorities, resources found, etc.

A. Determine scope

A1. *Review the regulatory environment to clarify the organization's jurisdiction and boundaries for change*
When you began the CBAETC journey, you started by reviewing your regulatory environment and your authority to make changes to accounting education and experience requirements. Before starting to design new program elements, your understanding of your organization's scope and boundaries should be revisited to ensure they are clearly understood.

For example, if your gap analysis documented a number of gaps in enabling competencies, there are a number of ways that a program can be modified to develop and assess these competencies in candidates, including program changes to education, exam/evaluation and experience elements. Before re-designing elements, you need to be clear on your authority to change each element.

A2. *Establish the scope of program elements to be re-designed (e.g., Some or all levels of IPD education, IPD training, and/or CPD)*
Ensure that the scope of your re-design is consistent with your jurisdiction. Based on your review in step A1 of this stage, set your scope accordingly.

For example, if your organization does not have the authority to change the experience requirements for professional accountants, you'll need to either work with the body that does have authority to make changes in that area, or you'll need to work within the realm of education and exams and limit your re-design to those elements.

Refine the scope by prioritizing the gaps documented in Stage 2, using the information from the Practice Analysis. The scope and pacing of your re-design is dependent on the resources you have available (human and financial). You should plan to close off all gaps as soon as possible, but if you need to spread the project out over time, your two key focus areas should be the competencies that were rated during the Practice Analysis as being:

1. Most important to protecting the public interest and responding to the most common needs of clients and employers; and
2. Essential to becoming a newly-certified professional accountant.

This includes both technical and enabling competencies. It may be tempting to focus only on technical gaps, but that would be grossly counterproductive—most organizations that do a full Practice Analysis have found that many enabling competencies are weighted as more important and essential than technical competencies by employers.

When determining your scope and priorities, pay attention to the gaps found in the current program as well as in the assessed competence level of practicing professional accountants.

For example, if your gap analysis showed that there are gaps in the competence of practicing members with respect to certain areas, you will want to include CPD in your scope, as this is the most likely way that these gaps can be closed. If competence gaps of practicing members were found to be significantly undermining the organization's public interest mandate, closing these gaps should be a high priority.

Consider gaps documented in Stage 2 that relate to a specialization. If your Competency Framework includes different competencies and/or proficiency levels for specializations such as audit, taxation advisory, or treasury management, remember to include your gap analyses for the specialization(s) when establishing your scope.

For example, if you have separate proficiency levels for attaining an audit license and gaps were found, your scope will need to include the program elements (pre- and/or post-certification) that are required to qualify for an audit license.

A3. Determine the extent to which other organizations will be partnered with

Determine if partnering is needed because of limited jurisdiction. If your organization does not have full and unlimited authorization over the elements of the certification program for professional accountants in your region, your best option for implementing change will likely be to partner with another body that does have the necessary authority. In Stage 1 (step A1), you would have initiated communication with these potential partners. In this Stage, you should solidify the commitment of partners with respect to developing and implementing changes.

Explore opportunities for local partnering to provide better use of collabora-tive resources. Some PAOs (such as the Institute of Chartered Accountants of Scotland), provide almost all aspects of professional accountancy education that lead to membership. Other PAOs (such as the SAICA) outsource all the necessary professional accountancy education to accredited universities, but retain responsibility for the qualifying examinations that—together with rel-evant practical experience—permit access to membership. For a detailed dis-cussion of the SAICA's approach, see appendix C. Still others (such as CPA Canada) take a hybrid approach to education by requiring an undergraduate degree and specific subject area coverage as admission criteria to a rigorous Professional Education Program that is maintained and administered by the PAO.

One of the best reasons for partnering on CBAETC projects is to make the most efficient use of limited resources in the local or regional environment. This can include partnerships between and among tertiary-level institutions and other learning/tuition providers, PAOs, and governments.

For example, if your organization is a PAO, consider partnering with one or more high-quality universities that can be accredited by the profession to pro-vide IPD. This type of partnership requires the university to be willing to work with the PAO to ensure that graduates are not only academically prepared for the workforce, but also have the practical skills and abilities to enter the professional program. In exchange, these universities (through advertising their accredited status) are better able to attract high-quality students who are pursuing careers as professional accountants.

Some jurisdictions have multiple PAOs. In these jurisdictions, different PAOs are sometimes given authority to service different sectors of the market (for example, one is authorized to certify audit professionals while another serves other professional accountants). It is efficient in these cases for there to be mutual recognition of qualifications among PAOs. For example, the PAO cer-tifying auditors should recognize other PAO's qualifications as a potential path-way to membership when combined with appropriate specialty courses and audit experience. Partnering on CBAETC initiatives can serve as the foundation for such agreements.

Don't overlook opportunities to partner with local governments or other organizations to build resources that can be used within the program.

The University of Cape Town's College of Accounting, for example, part-nered with online education provider GetSmarter to develop a set of high-quality accounting education resources. The project was funded by the Finance and Accounting Services Sector Education and Training Authority (FASSET) of South Africa and assisted by translators and presenters from Walter Sisulu University and WITS School of Accountancy. A series of free short videos explaining essential accounting topics have been made available to the public in English as well as in several local South Africa languages (see learnaccounting.uct.ac.za).

Evaluate potential opportunities for twinning or mentoring arrangements with a more established PAO or university. As previously mentioned, CBAETC is an area that most often requires making the use of expertise from experienced consultants. There may also be opportunities to draw on the expertise and assis-tance of a more experienced and established counterpart (PAO or university) to provide resources, ideas, and mentoring and support.

B. Design new elements and map competencies

B.1 Determine whether competency gaps in IPD should be filled using education, exams/evaluations and/or experience program elements

Back in Stage 1, as part of the Practice Analysis, you determined how a competency is best developed (through education, exams/evaluation and/or practical experience). Using this information, in conjunction with your gap analysis, designate where in the IPD program each competency that is not yet sufficiently covered should be addressed.

Note that most competencies should be developed and assessed through a combination of two or more program elements, particularly if they are required to be demonstrated at an Advanced proficiency level.

This is also the appropriate time to consider whether there are opportunities to more effectively and efficiently develop competencies even if they were deemed to be covered.

For example, you may have determined that communication competencies were deemed to be adequately developed during the required course elements through education and evaluations. If, however, your Practice Analysis determined that communication competencies should also be developed and evaluated through practical experience, there may be an opportunity to improve the effectiveness of competency assessment by adding specific requirements for supervisors to evaluate the communication skills of candidates during practical experience.

B2. Design accreditation program for tertiary-level education providers

The extent to which this step is relevant depends on whether your organization is responsible for the education program (as a university or PAO) or whether your organization is a PAO partnering with universities or training institutions and accrediting them to provide the initial and/or professional education.

When some or all of the accounting education leading to PAO membership is outsourced, it is essential that the PAO engage with those providing the outsourced services to ensure that they understand the detailed guidance on the competencies required for membership and that they make the necessary changes to their programs and teaching methods to effectively develop those competencies.

Review your current accreditation program. If your organization is a PAO that already accredits universities or other tertiary-level training institutions to provide IPD, you should review your accreditation program and determine if re-design is needed to ensure that the program allows partnerships with only those institutions that can effectively develop competence in aspiring professional accountants.

Research best-practice accreditation models. A key resource when designing accreditation programs is the guidance provided by AACSB International—The Association to Advance Collegiate Schools of Business. AACSB accredits institutions, business schools, and accounting academic units that:

- Demonstrate compliance with the AACSB accreditation standards
- Uphold the AACSB mission and core values
- Advance the interests of management and accounting education, and
- Participate in AACSB's global community of leading business schools and accounting programs.

AACSB focuses on "continuous quality improvement in management and accounting education through engagement, innovation, and impact." Accreditation is entirely voluntary, but is much sought-after in some environments, as it is seen as a stamp of quality and a means of attracting high-quality students and faculty, as well as international recognition.

Application for accreditation is open to business schools offering degrees in business administration. Accounting academic units (faculties, departments, etc.) can apply for an additional accreditation in accounting from AACSB. The two sets of standards are closely aligned, and the accounting accreditation is performed as an extension of the business accreditation process.

Accreditation is initially achieved through a process of self-evaluation and peer review, and is continued through periodic peer reviews. Guidance on the Business accreditation is available at: http://www.aacsb.edu/-/media/aacsb/docs/accreditation/standards/business-accreditation-2017-update.ashx?la=en.

Guidance on the accounting unit accreditation is found at: http://www.aacsb.edu/-/media/aacsb/docs/accreditation/standards/accounting-standards-2013-update.ashx?la=en

Other well-established accreditation systems should also be reviewed to guide your design work. For example:

- CPA Canada's accreditation and recognition standards for post-secondary institutions are available at: https://www.cpacanada.ca/en/become-a-cpa/pathways-to-becoming-a-cpa/national-education-resources/cpa-recognition-and-accreditation-standards
- Information on the SAICA's accreditation program is available at: https://www.saica.co.za/LearnersStudents/InformationonEducationProviders/InformationonAccreditedProgrammes/tabid/465/language/en-ZA/Default.aspx.

Commit to an accreditation model. An efficient model for accreditation programs relies on two levels or stages:

1. At the overall level, requirements should be in place to ensure the overall quality of instruction, rigor of assessment, and environment of active learning that supports and builds professionalism.
   Overall accreditation criteria could include:
   - Commitment to the profession
   - Faculty qualification and expertise
   - Sufficiency and educational involvement of faculty
   - Providing an appropriate learning environment
   - Inclusion of ethics policies
   - Inclusion of quality assurance policies
2. At the more detailed level, criteria should be in place to evaluate particular courses to ensure adequate content coverage, and development and assessment of relevant competencies at the expected proficiency levels.
   Specific exemption criteria could include:
   - Adequate content coverage, including both breadth and depth
   - Appropriate teaching and learning methodologies
   - Appropriate evaluation methodologies
   - Requiring acceptable minimum performance levels to achieve a Pass

Design a robust communication program for partner institutions. Outsourcing and partnering arrangements involving accreditation require a robust set of guidance documents to clearly articulate the expectations for program accreditation. Part of your design work should contemplate the set of documents that will be provided, and the formats of communication that will be used (such as manuals, online materials, blogs, Frequently Asked Questions [FAQs], templates, etc.).

Detailed guidance on the required competencies and proficiency levels is particularly important when a PAO outsources some, or all, of the accounting education and training that leads to PAO membership. This ensures education and training delivery agents can design and execute their programs appropriately.

B3. Design new education and exam/evaluation program elements mapped to the competency framework

If your organization maintains a program that provides IPD, your design documents for education elements should be in the form of curricula and syllabi, that guide education programs and specific courses. Exams and other evaluations should have blueprints that specify scope, allowable question styles and appropriate weightings for each.

Note that the AASCB accreditation standards are useful in the context of designing enhanced education and exam/evaluation program elements, even if AACSB accreditation is not being sought. PAOs who administer their own education program, and universities looking to increase the quality of their programs, can use the AACSB standards as a source of good practice for both general and specific design tips.

A note on terminology: when researching competency-based education, (particularly in the university context) you may come across the interpretation that competency-based education requires the use of an output-based approach, where qualifications are granted solely based on being able to pass evaluations, and progression is entirely self-paced. This is a valid approach, if the evaluations are rigorous enough and extensive enough to produce reliable results (in other words, if the evaluations are actually effective at differentiating competent candidates from those who are not competent, both from a technical and enabling competence perspective). The traditional model of tertiary education tends not to support a fully output-based approach because of the significant challenges in efficiently ensuring reliability. In a traditional setting, CBAETC is implemented within the normal structure of time-based semester schedules.

Fill technical competency gaps by adjusting technical domain course "streams" or "ladders." When designing additional coverage for technical competencies that are deemed to be best covered through education and exams/evaluations, it is often beneficial to consider the gap analysis of knowledge topics in the context of a stream or ladder of technical courses.

For example, in your IPD program, you likely require more than one financial accounting and reporting course. As part of your design, determine which of these courses should be augmented to fill any gaps you found. If your gap analysis determined significant gaps in this technical domain, you may need to add an additional course.

In the design stage, you should develop a document that shows where each knowledge topic is (and will be) covered within the technical course stream or ladder, including where intentional overlaps occur.

For example, the University of Cape Town develops allocation and "scaffolding" documents for course streams. In the domain of financial accounting and reporting, topic areas are listed based on the underlying accounting standards, and descriptions are provided of how each topic area is included in each financial accounting and reporting course in the stream. As an illustration, see the information provided by the scaffolding document with respect to coverage of IAS 2[7] (box 3.4).

Fill enabling competency gaps that are deemed to be best covered through education and exams/evaluations by designing active and effective teaching and learning methodologies. In the design stage, you should develop a document that shows where each enabling competency is (and will be) covered within the courses, and how they will be evaluated.

The development of enabling competencies is generally achieved by challenging candidates with a variety of active learning activities and assessments. These can include in-class discussions, debates, presentations, case studies and other simulations that require candidates to think critically, communicate logically, apply professional judgment and skepticism, and synthesize information. Similarly, evaluating enabling competencies requires that candidates demonstrate the application of judgment, critical thinking, communication, and ethics and professionalism skills to case studies and other realistic scenarios in assignments and on exams.

Because enabling competencies are meant to be applied across a broad range of contexts, it is important to ensure that the program be designed to include as many enabling competencies as possible within each of the program elements.

BOX 3.4

University of Cape Town financial reporting allocations and scaffolding

Assets
Inventory (IAS 2)
Course: Financial accounting
- importance of distinction between inventory and cost of sales
- when is an item recognized at cost
- at what amount is an item recognized at cost
- recording of inventory—perpetual and periodic methods
- cost allocation methods FIFO and Weighted average

Course: Financial reporting II
- identification of costs that should be allocated to inventory

- revision of formulas for determining cost of inventory
- conversion costs including overhead allocation
- dealing with changes in accounting policies for inventory (see IAS8 below)
- determination of net realizable value of inventory and dealing with write downs
- cost of inventory when transferred to branches/other divisions at transfer price (concept of reversing unrealized profits)
- disclosure requirements in respect of inventory

Courses: Financial reporting III & IV
- integration with other topics (e.g. foreign exchange transactions)

Determine whether exams/evaluations will be limited to single-subject on a course-by-course basis, or whether one or more integrative capstone evaluations will be used. Current best practice is to integrate the assessment of core competencies in a substantial, multidisciplinary IPD case study, generally offered as a capstone exam at the end of a professional program. Capstone exams require students to integrate concepts from several technical domains, as well as enabling competencies. For example, questions could require students to consider financial reporting, tax, and audit implications in a single question, while also being assessed on ethics and communication skills. Capstone exams often permit candidates to refer to technical resources during the exam—remember, recall of facts is not assessed at this level of the program.

These capstones assess whether aspiring professional accountants can:

- Apply their technical knowledge using higher-order critical thinking skills
- Make appropriate judgments in complex simulations of real-world facts and circumstances, and
- Proficiently communicate the relevant outputs.

These integrative exams are more effective than single-subject exams at assessing advanced levels of proficiency, but are also more difficult and expensive to develop, administer and mark. Resources and specific organizational priorities will need to be considered in determining how capstones should be designed into the program.

Design exam blueprints. The design of exams should be informed by the results of the Practice Analysis, and should reflect the ratings of competencies with respect to:

- Their importance in protecting the public and responding to the needs of clients and employers, and
- Their essentiality to becoming a newly-certified professional accountant.

Exam blueprints should specify, to the extent appropriate:

- Ranges for content areas within the course (e.g., 5–10 percent of assessment to be drawn from Module 1; 20–25 percent from Module 2 etc.)
- For multi-domain integrative exams, ranges of each domain to be represented (e.g., 25–35 percent of assessment to be drawn from Financial accounting and reporting competencies; 20–30 percent to be drawn from Assurance and audit competencies, etc.)
- Expectations for integrating enabling competencies (e.g., at least 25 percent of the assessment will be based on evaluation of enabling competencies)
- Acceptable question types and limits (e.g., at most 30 percent of assessment from multiple-choice questions; at least 40 percent from case simulations, etc.)
- For professional exams, the length of time over which full coverage of the Competency Framework is expected (e.g., all competencies intended to be assessed by examination should be covered at least once every 5 years).

Organizations new to this approach would benefit from consulting with experienced experts, including a psychometrician to address issues of exam validity and reliability.

Design a robust communication program for students/candidates. For exams/evaluations taken through university programs, students will often get adequate guidance and instruction from their professors. When PAOs administer professional exams, however, guidance documents need to be designed to help candidates prepare for exams, particularly because competency-based exams may be new to them.

This set of documents should include:

- Clear guidance on how to use the Competency Framework, Examination Blueprints, and so on, to support exam preparation
- Past or practice exams with sample solutions and grading guidance
- Comments from examiners/markers on past performance of exam writers, including common strengths and weaknesses.

B4. Design new practical experience program elements (e.g., Requirements, mentoring, review processes, documentation) mapped to Competency Framework

The practical experience program must synchronize efficiently and effectively with formal education and examination. In order to properly support developing and assessing competence, practical experience requirements typically contain five different types of program elements:

Determine minimum time requirements for practical experience. Minimum time requirements represent an input-based approach to developing competence, in that they measure time spent as opposed to objectives or outcomes achieved. Input requirements can be somewhat arbitrary, as candidates develop competence at different rates. It is preferable to use output-based approaches, which measure actual outcomes more directly. Unfortunately, output-based approaches tend to be challenging because they're more subjective to assess, whereas input-based approaches are easier to track and provide consistency. For these reasons, many organizations use a mix of input- and output-based approaches to ensure maximum reliability (figure 3.3).

For example, many organizations require candidates to obtain a minimum of 3 years of relevant work experience, in addition to demonstrating experience in specific competency domains. Some organizations grant credit towards the 3-year requirement for time spent in advanced education such as a Master's degree.

FIGURE 3.3
Minimum time requirements

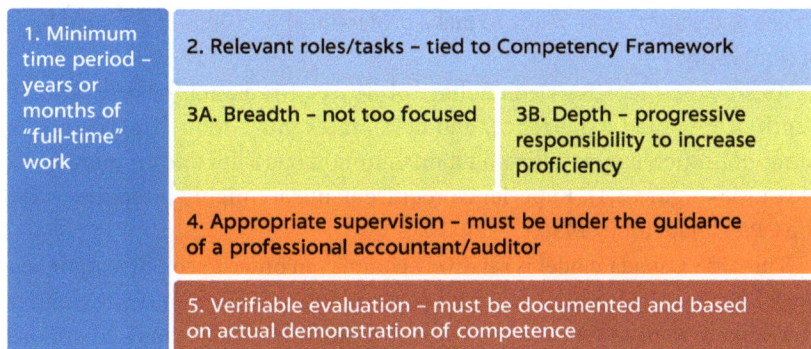

Candidates should be encouraged to undertake practical experience at the same time as completing their education requirements. Higher levels of competence are achieved when a candidate's theoretical learning in the classroom is directly enhanced by practical application on the job.

Before designing specific experience program elements, ensure your list of competencies (technical and enabling) expected to be developed and assessed in practical experience from step B1 of this Stage is complete. For technical competencies, experience is needed to provide opportunities for applying knowledge in a work context, thereby developing competence. Because candidates may choose different areas of focus within their practical experience requirements, many PAOs allow for flexibility in terms of specific technical competencies developed through experience, as long as the experience can be tied to the Competency Framework to ensure that the roles/tasks are relevant.

The competencies usually rated most essential to a newly designated professional accountant/auditor relate to professionalism, ethics and trust, leadership, and communications. Experience provides an outstanding opportunity to integrate various technical competencies, as well as integrating technical with enabling competencies. For most enabling competencies, it is necessary to ensure opportunities for them to be developed and assessed across practical experience as well as through education and exams/evaluations, particularly where an advanced level of proficiency is required. This is especially true for competencies that can only be demonstrated by an individual working as part of a team.

Determine breadth and depth requirements for roles and tasks undertaken during practical experience. **Breadth requirements** refer to the number of domains covered by a candidate during practical experience. **Depth requirements** refer to the focus or intensity of experience achieved within a domain. Breadth and depth requirements could include technical competencies (such as requiring a minimum number of assurance engagements to be completed) or enabling competencies (such as requiring that candidates progress to a supervisory position).

As mentioned in the previous point, most organizations recognize that candidates may choose to focus their careers in a particular domain within the profession. As a result, experience requirements often stipulate that certain core requirements be met with respect to the fundamental area of financial accounting and reporting, but otherwise allow flexibility of roles. Candidates are required to achieve acceptable breadth to support their overall professionalism and achieve an acceptable level of depth in a minimum number of areas of their choice to ensure they're ready to make professional decisions at the right level of complexity.

As an example, CPA Canada has robust requirements for breadth and depth of practical experience, and candidates must show progression in terms of proficiency by taking on more autonomous roles and/or more complex tasks (figure 3.4). Experience requirements are highly integrated with the CPA Competency Map.

This CPA Canada model is relatively complex in order to combine rigor and flexibility. Your own model may well be simpler, particularly at the beginning. You'll likely want to focus first on ensuring sufficient rigor, then add options to enhance flexibility once the system has been shown to be functioning effectively.

FIGURE 3.4

Requirements for breadth and depth of practical experience by CPA Canada

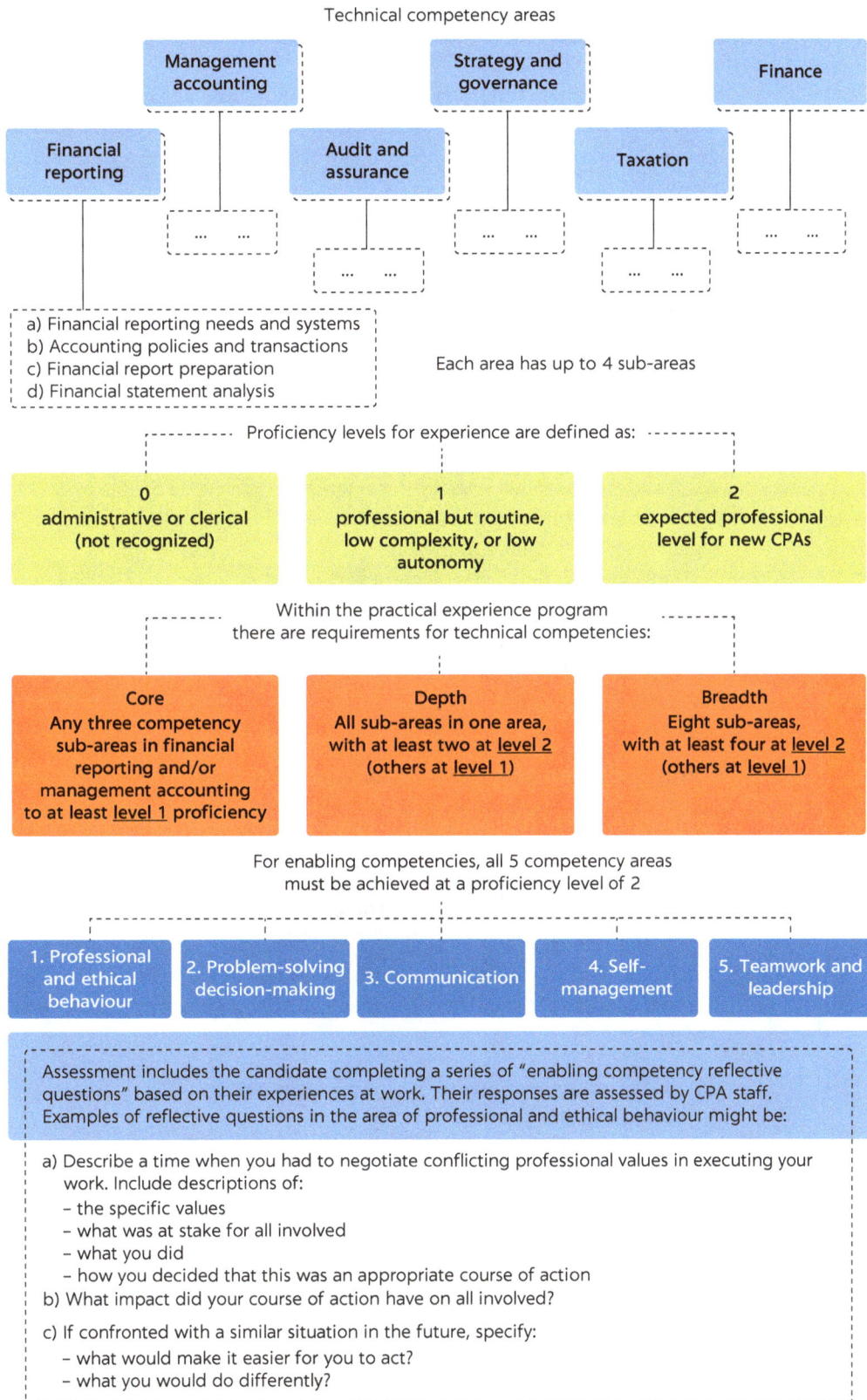

Technical competency areas

| Management accounting | | Strategy and governance | | Finance |

| Financial reporting | | Audit and assurance | | Taxation | |

... ...

a) Financial reporting needs and systems
b) Accounting policies and transactions
c) Financial report preparation
d) Financial statement analysis

Each area has up to 4 sub-areas

Proficiency levels for experience are defined as:

| **0** administrative or clerical (not recognized) | **1** professional but routine, low complexity, or low autonomy | **2** expected professional level for new CPAs |

Within the practical experience program there are requirements for technical competencies:

| **Core** Any three competency sub-areas in financial reporting and/or management accounting to at least level 1 proficiency | **Depth** All sub-areas in one area, with at least two at level 2 (others at level 1) | **Breadth** Eight sub-areas, with at least four at level 2 (others at level 1) |

For enabling competencies, all 5 competency areas must be achieved at a proficiency level of 2

| 1. Professional and ethical behaviour | 2. Problem-solving decision-making | 3. Communication | 4. Self-management | 5. Teamwork and leadership |

Assessment includes the candidate completing a series of "enabling competency reflective questions" based on their experiences at work. Their responses are assessed by CPA staff. Examples of reflective questions in the area of professional and ethical behaviour might be:

a) Describe a time when you had to negotiate conflicting professional values in executing your work. Include descriptions of:
   – the specific values
   – what was at stake for all involved
   – what you did
   – how you decided that this was an appropriate course of action
b) What impact did your course of action have on all involved?

c) If confronted with a similar situation in the future, specify:
   – what would make it easier for you to act?
   – what you would do differently?

Source: CPA Canada. Used with permission; further permission required for reuse.
Note: More information on the CPA Canada Practical Experience requirements and examples of reflective questions can be found at https://www.cpacanada.ca/en/become-a-cpa/cpa-designation-practical-experience-requirements-overview.

Determine mentoring or supervisory requirements. During practical experience, appropriate supervision by a qualified member of the profession is essential. Requirements could include regular meetings with mentors and requiring that the supervisor formally assess competence and provide feedback on a regular basis to the candidate.

Remember that employers are generally busy and are not likely to be familiar with competency assessment techniques. As a result, you'll need to design requirements that are efficient and easy to follow, or else they will be resisted.

Determine evaluation and documentation requirements. Formal evaluation of competence (technical and enabling) is often more challenging with respect to experience requirements than it is with respect to education and examination requirements. It's essential, however, that competence achieved through experience be properly documented as part of the PAO's certification processes.

During a candidate's work experience, reviews must be performed regularly to ensure progress is being made, and at the end to ensure requirements are met. Results of these reviews must be documented to provide verifiable evidence. When designing enhanced requirements, you'll need to specify frequency of reports, sign-offs required, and so on.

Many organizations rely, at least in part, on self-assessment of competence performed by candidates. As a result, and because it can be challenging to achieve consistency in competency assessment from a broad range of mentors, supervisors, and employers, it is good practice for PAOs to have an audit process for candidate experience records.

Using approved training offices/organizations

Many organizations find it efficient to pre-approve specific positions or roles at certain employing organizations. Approved organizations are evaluated by the PAO in advance to ensure that they are committed to developing competent professionals, and that they are capable of providing appropriate depth and breadth of experience to candidates. Candidates in these approved training offices are generally subject to less rigorous documentation requirements because the PAO has confidence in the working environment and the experience program being undertaken.

B5. Design new CPD elements (e.g., Requirements, courses) mapped to Competency Framework

IAESB's IES 7 requires that IFAC member bodies:

- Make CPD mandatory for all professional accountants
- Promote the importance of, and commitment to, CPD
- Facilitate access to CPD
- Establish an approach to CPD measurement, and
- Monitor and enforce CPD requirements.

The requirements in this Standard should inform your work when designing new CPD elements.

Note that at the time of publication of this Guide, IES 7 is undergoing extensive revision. Be mindful of any substantive changes to the requirements.

Determine if changes should focus on new requirements, new course offerings, or both. The new elements required will depend on the gaps identified in your gap analysis. If a general lack of confidence in members' abilities was found, you'd need to consider an overall increase in CPD requirements. This may include imposing greater structure on CPD undertaken and/or increasing the requirements for ensuring that approved CPD providers offer sufficiently rigorous courses to be effective in increasing competence.

For example, if your gap analysis indicated that practicing members are not meeting competence requirements with respect to their ability to apply the PAO's code of professional conduct, you may decide to impose a requirement for mandatory training on the code of conduct to increase members' awareness and ability to apply the code's requirements.

On the other hand, if the gap analysis uncovered that the key concerns were limited to specific technical areas, you would likely choose to address this by designing expanded resources in the areas found to be lacking.

For example, if your analysis showed that there were few professional accountants with expertise in finance, you may decide to expand the course offerings in that area.

Decide if an output-based, input-based, or combination approach to CPD reporting and maintenance will be used. **Output-based approaches** specify requirements in terms of learning outcomes achieved (e.g., requiring professional accountants to determine their individual learning and development needs; completing learning activities to meet those needs; and demonstrating learning outcomes through reflective activities and verified demonstration of learning, such as completion of an assessment).

Input-based approaches specify requirements in terms of the amount of learning activities required, often measured in hours or other learning units (e.g., requiring 120 hours of CPD, of which 60 hours must be verifiable, over a 3-year rolling cycle).

Combination approaches combine elements of input and output-based approaches (e.g., requiring professional accountants to complete a certain number of hours of learning activities and document actual learning outcomes through reflective activities.)

Output-based approaches to measuring CPD are most consistent with CBAETC because their design requires demonstrating the attainment and maintenance of specified competencies; however, these approaches can be more challenging to administer due to their more subjective measurement nature.

Consider if changes are needed for CPD related to specialist roles. Depending on the results of your gap analysis, the changes you design may apply to all professional accountants or to only those in specialist roles such as auditors or tax advisors.

C. Develop new program elements and update mappings

Once you have designs in place that show how competency gaps will be corrected through enhancements to education, exam/evaluation, experience, and CPD requirements, your next step is to develop the new program elements.

As you develop elements, be sure to update your mapping documents that link the program elements to your Competency Framework.

It is essential that the focus be on developing competence though the use of appropriate teaching and learning methodologies that are pedagogically sound. This is an area where organizations new to CBAETC may find it particularly valuable to work with educators experienced in the field.

An important resource when developing program elements is the guidance on implementing a learning outcomes approach, provided by the IAESB (see https://www.ifac.org/publications-resources/guidance-support-implementation-learning-outcomes-approach). A learning outcomes approach focuses on the candidate's ability to demonstrate achieving the learning outcomes at the required level of proficiency, rather than on the learning process. In other words, this approach aims to directly develop and assess competence, specifically as related to the learning outcomes required by the IESs.

Remember that when you developed your Competency Framework, one of the key requirements was to cover the learning outcomes specified in the IESs.

C1. Develop new education and exam/evaluation program elements to develop and assess competence

Develop new course materials based on design documents. Develop new materials to cover any knowledge topics that were found to be missing. Remember to keep the proficiency levels in mind and focus on competence, not knowledge recall. Candidates should understand the rationale, principles, and conceptual frameworks that underpin the material.

Most reputable textbooks will approach learning based on developing competence, specifying learning outcomes that reflect appropriate levels of proficiency for the material being covered. When selecting textbooks, match the proficiency level reflected in the textbook against the proficiency level that is required to be developed. For consistency, and to ensure appropriate overlap is designed in, streams of courses in the same domain should be (re)developed as a set.

Recognizing that students have different learning styles, consideration should be given to using different presentation mediums for content delivery. As an example of innovative material that targets competence rather than simply knowledge, consider the LearnAccounting videos developed by the University of Cape Town College of Accounting (available at http://learnaccounting.uct.ac.za—free account required). Even in the basic-level financial reporting videos, the focus is on understanding how a business works and why reporting systems are needed, rather than on memorizing the accounting equation or memorizing definitions of debits and credits. As a specific example, in the video on Understanding Debits and Credits, the professor explains why students are often confused by debits and credits, by walking through how typical transactions with a bank would be recorded from the perspectives of both the bank and the individual.

With respect to specifically developing course material in financial accounting and reporting, competency-based materials can be developed through a focus on framework-based teaching, discussed in depth in appendix C.

Because the objective of the Conceptual Framework is to facilitate the consistent and logical formulation of IFRSs, adopting a Framework-based approach to teaching IFRSs provides students with a cohesive understanding of IFRSs by relating the requirements in IFRSs to the objective of IFRS financial information and the concepts that underlie IFRSs and inform its development. That understanding should enhance the ability of students to exercise the judgments that are necessary to apply IFRSs and should better prepare them to update continuously their IFRS knowledge and competencies in the context of life-long learning (Wells 2011).

Framework-based teaching adheres to the following ideas:

- Educators should focus on ensuring that students understand the key principles that underpin the topics being discussed
- Students should be taught to evaluate why a technique is used, or why a technique is inappropriate, as opposed to focusing on the mechanics of how to apply techniques. This will allow them to develop a stronger understanding of the particular topic and the subject as a whole, and aid in their ability to apply techniques in new situations
- A good lecture will result in a student understanding the basic principles that need to be applied in dealing with that topic, and how that topic fits into the broader subject matter. A poor lecture, by contrast, will result in a student learning disconnected concepts and techniques without an appreciation of the bigger picture.

Such teaching methods necessarily emphasize clearly communicating the research, analysis, and well-reasoned arguments that explain the judgments made in reaching clearly documented conclusions about relevant real-world tasks or simulations thereof. On the other hand, memory recall and mechanical examples are de-emphasized because in today's environment they are of little value to the work of a professional accountant. Consequently, open-book teaching, learning, and assessment is wholly consistent with CBAETC. Appendix A provides an example of how the University of Cape Town College of Accounting's financial reporting staff implemented framework-based teaching in conjunction with SAICA's move to CBAETC.

To support teachers in developing their students' abilities to make IFRS® Standards judgments and estimates, the IASB's Education Initiative provides IFRS® Standards teachers with free-to-download Framework-based teaching material (in several languages), including comprehensive case studies with accompanying detailed teaching notes (available at: http://www.ifrs.org /academics/framework-based-teaching-material/).

The discussion of framework-based teaching in appendix C includes a variety of education and evaluation techniques to ensure that students are focusing on the principles. Although these are presented in the context of framework-based teaching for accounting, these techniques are valuable beyond the domain of financial accounting and reporting and should be applied across the education program. Of particular importance is the recommendation to challenge students with unfamiliar situations and include irrelevant information in questions to ensure that they are applying the principles and not just following a predetermined set of steps.

Your new course material should include a variety of activities that engage students in active discussion, analysis, and evaluation of principles and concepts. At the same time, in-class activities need to emphasize the development of enabling competencies such as critical thinking and judgement, professionalism and ethics, communication, teamwork and leadership.

Relevant activities include case discussions, presentations, research, and group projects.

Develop new exam/evaluation materials based on your design documents. As previously emphasized, ensuring that the required proficiency level has been achieved cannot be done without examining or evaluating the material at that proficiency level. Competency-based evaluations of formal education can take a variety of forms, including final projects, presentations or oral exams, and written exams. For objectivity, it is generally preferred to have the most significant portion of a student's final grade be determined by written exams and individually-prepared written submissions.

When developing exams, ensure compliance with the exam blueprint prepared in the design step. This document will guide your coverage of the appropriate competencies at the required proficiency levels, using the desired question formats.

If multiple-choice questions are included, be sure to draft them in such a way as to require higher-order skills, rather than the rote memorization that is typical of knowledge-based questions (box 3.5).

Similarly, with short-answer questions, be sure to avoid questions that only require repeating memorized information (box 3.6).

To evaluate competencies at an advanced level of proficiency, and to integrate a range of technical competencies with enabling competencies, case study questions and simulations are usually the most effective and efficient. These questions require candidates to consider different perspectives and apply

---

BOX 3.5

Sample multiple-choice questions

Compare the following two multiple-choice questions:

Question A:
What type of threat to independence is most likely to occur when an auditor has been working with a client for many years?

1. Self-interest
2. Familiarity
3. Self-review
4. Intimidation

Question B:
You have been engaged by XYZ Corporation for the past 6 years to perform the company's audit and tax work. XYZ is an important client to your firm, as it provides around 5 percent of your revenues, and XYZ's management has recommended you to several other large clients. As the audit work is concluding, you have run into a serious disagreement with the CFO about how to account for and disclose an event. The CFO says to you "We've known each other a long time, and I expect you to respect my judgment here. I get calls regularly from other auditors wanting this engagement. I'd hate to think that I've been foolish in staying loyal to you and referring my colleagues to you as well."

What types of threats to independence are most evidenced here?

1. Familiarity and self-interest
2. Self-interest and intimidation
3. Intimidation and self-review
4. Self-review and familiarity

The difference should be obvious to you; Question A can be memorized from a textbook, whereas Question B requires application, judgment, and prioritization.

BOX 3.6

Short-answer questions

On an exam, a student is asked to explain inherent and control risks, including characteristics or situations that would increase or decrease the risks.

This is primarily a knowledge-based question, as the student can memorize the two types of risk, what they mean, and the common indicators of risk being lower or higher.

A better approach (to assess a higher proficiency level) would be to give the student a description of a company and ask them to evaluate the inherent risk and control risk and identify which balances and/or cycles of transactions are the most concerning for this particular company from an audit perspective.

This second variation of the question is much more competency-based and requires a higher proficiency level to respond appropriately. The answer will depend on the specifics of the company, and judgment will be required to prioritize issues.

---

concepts and techniques in uncertain and unfamiliar situations. Case studies are particularly useful when developing capstone exams.

If developing competency-based exams and evaluations is new to you, you will want to review a variety of examples of good- and best-practice exams available from well-established institutions. For example:

- CPA Canada's Common Final Examination simulations and guides are available at: https://www.cpacanada.ca/en/become-a-cpa/cpa-certification -program-evaluation/the-common-final-examination-report-simulations -and-guides-for-the-cfe
- SAICA's Initial Test of Competence (ITC): past exams are available at https:// www.saica.co.za/LearnersStudents/Examinations/ExamInformation /PastExamPapers/PartIQualifyingExamination/tabid/1168/language /en-ZA/Default.aspx
- SAICA's Assessment of Professional Competence (APC): past exams are available at: https://www.saica.co.za/LearnersStudents/Examinations /ExamInformation/PastExamPapers/AssessmentofProfessional CompetencePartIIQ/tabid/3629/language/en-ZA/Default.aspx
- ACCA study support resources, including specimen exams are available at: http://www.accaglobal.com/gb/en/student/exam-support-resources.html.

Develop communication documents for candidates. Initial documentation should provide guidance on how to prepare for competency-based exams, and should provide examples of how the Competency Framework and exam blueprints should be used in exam preparation.

CPA Canada, for example, provides a broad range of guidance to candidates on preparing for the Common Final Evaluation (including guidance on how to use the blueprint and the CPA Competency Map for exam preparation) at: https://www.cpacanada.ca/en/become-a-cpa/cpa-certification-program -evaluation/cpa-certification-capstone-1-cfe-cases

In the design step, it was noted that past exams and examiners' comments on past performance are important documents. For new exams that have not yet been written, it is best practice to provide "sample" exams and solutions that mirror the format and expectations of the actual exam.

See the links to past exams above for examples of communication to candidates on exam preparation and examiner comments on candidate performance.

C2. Develop or update accreditation policies for tertiary-level education providers

Develop administrative tools to support the new accreditation program. Based on the accreditation model you specified in the design stage, develop accreditation standards, processes, forms, and templates. Re-examine the AASCB guidance documentation and other PAO accreditation programs you researched during the design phase.

Develop communication and guidance documents. In addition to standards and templates, you should also develop specific communications for various stakeholders, such as potential accreditation partners and students attending accredited universities.

Accreditation partners need to understand how their work ties in with the work of others (i.e., they need to clearly understand their responsibilities in the context of the bigger picture). Students attending accredited universities need to understand how their university education fits in with the balance of requirements for becoming a professional accountant.

C3. Develop new practical experience program elements to develop and assess competence

Develop administrative tools to support new requirements. Based on your design decisions in step B4, you will likely need to develop administrative materials to support enhanced practical experience requirement policies. These will include:

- Reporting templates for documenting candidates' progress, and
- Internal administrative documents to evaluate, approve, and monitor approved training offices.

Develop communication and guidance documents. These will include:

- Guides for candidates and employers
- FAQs, and
- Samples of completed templates such as applications for becoming an approved training office/organization and candidate assessment.

Focus on key documents and build resources over time. Examples from well-established organizations include:

- CPA Canada provides substantial guidance for employers and candidates (including information on competency requirements and mentorship) at https://www.cpacanada.ca/en/become-a-cpa/cpa-designation-practical-experience-requirements-overview
- SAICA provides a wide range of guidance and forms for trainees and training organizations (including a range of up-to-date assessment resources, assessment instruments, and generic training plans to support efficiency and effectiveness in the execution of its practical experience requirements) at https://www.saica.co.za/Training/Training/tabid/411/language/en-ZA/Default.aspx.

C4. Develop new CPD program elements to help close competence gaps in existing professionals

Develop administrative tools to support new CPD requirements. If new CPD requirements have been designed, such as introducing mandatory courses or output-based measures, these requirements will create a need for new forms, templates, and reporting mechanisms.

Develop and/or outsource the development of new courses required to fill competency gaps. In the design step, you outlined the courses that need to be developed or revised. For those courses where internal expertise is available, you may want to develop them in-house. For other courses, it may be more effective to outsource the course development to subject matter experts. For outsourced courses, be sure that the developer has a full understanding of the competencies to be covered and the proficiency levels required.

When developing technical CPD courses, do not overlook opportunities to help members develop enabling competencies as well. For example, small group discussions, case studies, and other interactive techniques can increase the level of engagement in CPD sessions, and help members enhance their communication, critical thinking, analysis and teamwork skills.

Develop communication and guidance documents. As with other elements, effective communication will be necessary to ensure that the changes are understood and accepted by those who will be affected by them.

C5. Update all mappings

For every new program element, review both during and at the end of development work to ensure that the intended competency gaps have been closed (or to what extent they have been closed). Keep mapping documents up-to-date as new elements are developed and update future work plans for gaps that could not yet be filled.

D. Train instructors and trainers

D1. Select instructors and trainers with experience and/or aptitude in competency-based methods

When first embarking on CBAETC, you will likely not have many instructors available in-house who are experienced in competency-based education methods, though undoubtedly most will be adaptable to this approach. If similar organizations in your region have previously implemented CBAETC, you may be able to enlist experienced individuals to assist. If this is not an option, it may be necessary to hire experienced consultants to help select and train instructors with aptitudes that will allow them to succeed in CBAETC.

Note that, oftentimes, instructors with the most aptitude for CBAETC are those that are considered innovative and most comfortable with change. It is important that they have enough experience in teaching to be confident in the classroom and be respected by their peers to effectively champion the approach.

D2. Involve instructors and trainers in the development and/or review of materials to maximize buy-in and familiarity

Once instructors have been identified, it is important to get them involved in the process as early and fully as possible. This allows them to become immersed in the language and methodologies of CBAETC, and generates buy-in to the initiative while building expertise.

D3. Hold formal training sessions and provide resources for competency-based instruction

The goal here is to develop a team of educators who are comfortable with—and competent in—CBAETC methods. Initial training sessions can be provided by experienced external consultants, but initial training should be designed as "train-the-trainer" sessions, so that further dissemination can be done more quickly and so that active knowledge transfer enhances long-term, internal program sustainability.

Milestones of success

You have now created an overall design for your new program, supported by a complete set of new and revised program elements to bridge the gaps between your current programs and systems and your Competency Framework. These new elements may cover any or all of education, exams, practical experience and CPD.

Your design and development documents include mapping of all new elements back to your Competency Framework, and these mappings will be maintained going forward so that you can always see the direct linkage between your programs and the expected competence of professional accountants in your jurisdiction.

You are now ready to implement your new program elements.

A CONDENSED APPROACH TO STAGE 3: DESIGN AND DEVELOP AN EXPANDED PROGRAM

If your organization has been using a condensed approach to CBAETC, your gap analysis may be anecdotal, as opposed to including a full mapping of existing program elements to the Competency Framework and resulting gaps. This may lead to less structured design steps, with more reliance being placed on the expertise of program element developers to prioritize changes and additions.

If resources are tight, such prioritization is vital. You should:

- Focus first on core elements, such as foundational and advanced courses in fundamental domains, and be sure to place sufficient emphasis on developing and assessing enabling competencies
- Use outsourcing and partnerships to increase efficient resource use, but consider limiting partnerships to trusted organizations that require relatively little vetting (such as top-tier universities and larger accounting firms and companies)
- Develop key documents, tools and templates initially, and grow your database of resources over time
- Keep control of essential elements for assessing competence, such as a final capstone exam and practical experience sign-offs
- Hire experts and/or locate twinning opportunities to harness expertise to learn from as well as gaining resources to build upon.

Regardless of whether a condensed approach has been used in other stages, it is imperative that development on expanded elements focus on developing of competence in both technical and enabling competencies, and that the resulting revised program be fully mapped to the Competency Framework. Without this mapping, there will be no way to manage the program, assess enhancements, and undertake continuous improvement.

STAGE 4: IMPLEMENT THE EXPANDED PROGRAM

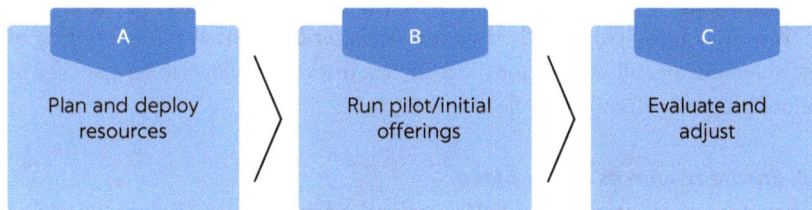

Now comes the exciting part—putting the new pieces in place. Plan your launch carefully, but be ready to adjust as you go—as you learn how to implement the process in your own environment.

A. Plan and deploy resources

A1. Determine the desired timeline and the launch approach to be used

Determine which elements would benefit from a pilot launch. For new or heavily revised program elements that are large and resource intensive, it may be beneficial to pilot the new elements with a small group of students, members, or other stakeholders prior to undertaking a full launch. This can help contain the exposure and allow the team to work out any important issues before launching broadly. A pilot can also provide an opportunity to schedule more extensive feedback sessions from a relatively small group, so that rich feedback can be obtained while keeping the amount of feedback easier to manage and address.

For example:

- A new course or exam could be piloted with a small group of students
- A new accreditation program could be piloted with one or two respected universities; and
- A new practical experience mentoring program could be piloted with one or two respected employers.

Where pilot offerings are used, it may be beneficial to offer the opportunity for participants to take part at no cost (e.g., by waiving course/exam or CPD fees) in exchange for committing to providing regular and in-depth feedback throughout the pilot.

Set target launch dates for new elements. When rolling out new elements, be careful not to try to launch all items at once. Instead, choose a logical starting point and plan for a progression that staggers your launches, so that you have an opportunity to fine-tune along the way and ensure elements stay coordinated. Using natural cycles of program elements can help and will make their implementation less disruptive.

For example, you may wish to launch the pilot or initial offering of new or revised courses at the beginning of the academic year or when such courses are normally offered, with new exams following at the end of the semester.

New CPD requirements may be best launched to coincide with the beginning of a new reporting period, to give members time to adjust.

Set a schedule for check-ins and reviews, and for feedback to be addressed. Every new program element will need some fine-tuning along the way, so it's important to schedule interim check-in points. Stakeholders should be provided with incentives to provide feedback in order to get the broadest perspectives possible.

You should also plan to schedule reviews after the pilot or initial offering of each element and allow time for the feedback from the reviews to be disposed of before the next offering or cycle.

A2. Ensure resources are in place

For new courses, exams, and CPD sessions, ensure that sufficient, qualified instructors/facilitators have been retained. In the previous stage, you began training instructors, and included them in the development work of new courses and exams/evaluations. You also engaged staff or consultants to develop enhanced CPD materials. In this Stage, connect with the instructors and facilitators who will be involved in the first sessions to ensure that they are prepared, confident, and ready to start.

For new courses, exams, and CPD sessions, arrange sufficient, appropriate venues. Course and exam venues are often arranged in conjunction with local universities, even if they're being fully administered by the PAO. Care should be taken to ensure that the venues chosen remain convenient for the students/candidates.

CPD sessions are often held at hotels and conference centers, but if resources are constrained, there may be opportunities to hold these sessions at local schools, universities, community centers, or the PAO's own offices to reduce costs.

For new practical experience requirements, sufficiently prepare employers and supervisors. Those responsible for overseeing practical experience should have adequate guidance and reference materials to meet the requirements, and should be prepared to answer questions from trainees. Consider holding training sessions or webinars to inform employers of the changes and address their concerns.

Ensure that in-house staff have sufficient resources to manage the increased administrative burden that will result from the changes. Staff need to be prepared not only to manage their own workload, but also to manage the increase in questions and feedback from stakeholders that will likely result from launching the new program elements.

Ensure there are sufficient resources dedicated to communications, project management, and change management. Launching new program elements will likely represent a significant change for your organization and for stakeholders impacted by the new requirements. Achieving buy-in will require that there be sufficient time and effort spent on ensuring that stakeholders are kept informed, and that they feel adequately supported during the transition. Success in this area will depend on:

- Starting your communication plan as early as possible, to include and engage those who have not been part of the project to date
- Having clear messaging on the need for change and the decisions made (draw on your research, your Practice Analysis results, and gap analysis to help with this messaging)
- Having prepared appropriate communications and guidance for stakeholders, and
- Ensuring that staff, instructors, and others involved in delivering the new program be given adequate time and support to maintain documentation and communications along the way.

Given the magnitude of the project, you may want to consider hiring a change-management expert to oversee and coordinate efforts or explicitly adding such responsibilities to an existing staff member's job description.

A3. Run pilot/initial offerings of education and exam/evaluation program elements
Run the first sessions of new courses and exams/evaluations. Ensure that instructors are adequately supported during the process. Support ideas include the following:

- Ensure adequate administrative support
- Consider setting up regular discussion times for facilitators to give feedback
- Ensure that instructors teaching different courses have a means of communicating with, and supporting each other during the first offerings
- Provide facilitators with an experienced competency-based educator they can get advice from quickly when needed.

Collect feedback. Collect feedback as per the interim check-in schedule and on an ad-hoc basis as provided. The feedback should be classified to determine which comments can be addressed immediately, and which are better to defer until the next offering or cycle. You may also wish to prioritize feedback as essential, important, or nice-to-have and then allocate your resources accordingly.

A4. Initialize new practical experience program elements
Launch new requirements. Ensure that candidates/trainees and employers are aware of the effective dates for changes and remind them of where to find resources and get help when they need it. Ensure that documentation is clear and easy to understand what the new requirements are, how and when reporting is completed, each party's responsibilities, and whether reporting is subject to a verification or audit process by the PAO. It is helpful to develop a FAQ document to anticipate the most common queries from stakeholders.

Collect feedback. Collect feedback as per the interim check-in schedule and on an ad-hoc basis as provided. As above, the feedback should be classified to determine which comments can be addressed immediately and which are better to defer until the next offering or cycle, as well as any other prioritization deemed appropriate.

A5. Initialize and run pilot/initial offerings of CPD program elements

Launch new requirements. Ensure that members (including those subject to any changes in specialist requirements) are aware of the effective dates for changes and remind them of where to find resources and get help when they need it. As with the practical experience changes, developing a FAQ document is a beneficial step in effective change management and to reduce the administrative burden on staff fielding similar questions on repeated occasions.

Run the first sessions of new CPD course offerings. Ensure that facilitators have access to adequate administrative support. If requirements for CPD reporting or compliance have also changed, ensure facilitators are prepared to answer questions about the requirement changes. If possible, have PAO staff attend at least one of each of the new CPD offerings to better understand the course and its impact, as well as the feedback received.

Collect feedback. Collect feedback after each session. As above, the feedback should be classified to determine which comments can be addressed for the next offering, and which are better to defer until the next cycle.

There are numerous no cost or low cost online survey tools available that can be used to both increase response rates, by lowering the effort required to respond, as well as providing some basic analytical tools to summarize feedback more efficiently.

Consider incentivizing feedback to further increase feedback response rates. Subject to any gaming regulations you may have to comply with, entering respondents into a draw for a free or discounted CPD course or some other prize often works well.

B. Evaluate and adjust

B1. Monitor, document and assess results

Compile and evaluate feedback on pilot/initial offerings. In Step A1, you set up a schedule for reviews and interim check-ins. During, and at the completion of, the pilot or initial offerings, be sure that the feedback is systematically compiled and adequately evaluated.

When analyzing feedback, it is important to consider the source of feedback and potential underlying motivations. Be aware that some stakeholders will be resistant to the change, and their perception of the change may be clouded by that resistance. Nonetheless, make sure you maintain an open mind to all feedback, regardless of the source, as valid concerns may still be the basis of even biased feedback.

Celebrate successes. A key part of managing change is to recognize successes and acknowledge the hard work that made them happen. Focusing on the "wins" helps to make the small setbacks along the way more manageable and such recognition can be a powerful, intangible motivator for key stakeholders and contributors.

Determine necessary adjustments. No new element will be perfect the first time offered. Based on the feedback received and your own evaluation and analysis of new elements, determine adjustments necessary to adapt and improve processes, materials, and guidance. Be careful, however, not to plan radical changes unless you are certain they are necessary. It's generally more successful in the long run to adjust gradually and systematically, to allow time for the effectiveness of changes to be evaluated.

Also be aware that in some situations where negative feedback has been encountered, the solution may be better communication, guidance, or setting of expectations as opposed to actually making adjustments to the new elements. This is especially true in situations where stakeholders are exhibiting resistance. Balance the need for program adjustments with the need for better change management.

B2. Make adjustments to program elements

Once you have determined the adjustments that are necessary to the new elements, these adjustments should be made systematically and reviewed by competent reviewers to ensure that the adjustments have been carried out appropriately. Where changes are made, undertake a careful review to identify where conforming changes may be necessary to other program elements as a result.

B3. Update mapping to competency framework

As elements are revised, it is imperative that the mapping documents that link the elements to the Competency Framework be updated to reflect the changes. Efficient mapping will likely need to be undertaken by the subject-matter experts (staff or consultants) working on the revisions in conjunction with individuals most experienced with your Competency Framework.

B4. Report to stakeholder groups

An important part of your communications plan should be a structured report to key stakeholders. Although ongoing communications with stakeholders should have been carried out regularly through the implementation of new elements, it is important to periodically provide more formal and structured updates to ensure that everyone is adequately informed of progress to date and future plans. This step is particularly important where you have existing reporting relationships with certain stakeholders, such as government or oversight bodies.

Regular communication helps to emphasize successes and create and maintain momentum for continuing revisions and changes.

B5. Establish continuous review and improvement process

In a world where change is constant, a PAO must continuously review and periodically recalibrate its accounting education, training, and certification to ensure that its members are capable of providing the services the market needs. As business and accounting evolve, PAOs must respond.

Determine the timeline for regular review cycles. All program elements should be reviewed on a regular basis beginning with the Competency Framework, and following through Stages 2 through 4, to the extent warranted based on the extent of change in the competencies and/or proficiency levels.

Given the pace of change in the accounting profession, it is important that the Competency Framework be evaluated at least every few years to ensure that it remains current and relevant. If a full Practice Analysis was performed originally, and if the organization has sufficient resources, re-performing the Practice Analysis can be the most effective method of ensuring continued rigor. If the organization does not wish to (or is unable to) allocate resources to a new Practice Analysis, using a condensed approach can still be effective. Regardless of the approach chosen:

- Ensure that the review is planned and completed systematically, with ideas, observations, and resolutions being well-documented
- Choose your review team carefully—you need a balance of individuals who are well-versed in the current Competency Framework and its application, as well as business leaders and visionaries with a keen perception of business trends and the competencies needed to manage them
- Keep longevity in mind—it is often tempting to write competency statements specific to the issue of the day, but try to phrase your statements to convey meaning that will not become dated too quickly. For example, referring to "emerging technologies such as cryptocurrencies and artificial intelligence" will become dated as soon as these technologies are mainstream. A longer-lasting reference would be to "digital technologies such as cryptocurrencies and artificial intelligence"
- Remember that you are changing a fundamental and foundational piece of your organization's programs: be thorough and ensure adequate follow-through, including communication of changes to those who use the Framework or are impacted by it.

Reviews of individual elements can be done by revisiting all elements at once every few years, or staggering reviews such that they are spread throughout a 3–5 year cycle. To decide on the approach to use, prioritize based on the review and analysis of the Competency Framework and the resulting changes. For example, if the Framework was revised to put more emphasis on risk management, there will likely be gaps that need to be filled. For efficiency, you'd want to prioritize your review and update of the courses and other elements in the program where risk management competencies are developed and assessed.

Appendix C provides an illustration of the AICPA's continuous review process.

As reviews are completed on individual elements, consider how the findings impact other elements as well. This requires ensuring there are adequate feedback loops that include a specific mechanism for determining what other elements are affected by any issues noted and adjustments proposed. As such, the review process for individual elements should involve a reviewer or oversight of someone who has a broader understanding of all program elements and how they interact.

Continue building relevant resources. In order for your CBAETC initiatives to be sustainable, it is important to continue recruiting and training instructors, facilitators, subject matter experts, and administrative staff. Is also important to consider succession planning for those in leadership positions who have been responsible for the initial implementation. Implementing CBAETC is a significant undertaking, and you should ensure that new and emerging leaders are encouraged to carry the initiative forward.

Monitor relevant trends. In order to prepare for the future, continue scanning for relevant trends, as you did in Stage I (Step A2). The program needs to continue to reflect the context and challenges faced by professional accountants.

As part of this scanning, it is beneficial to subscribe to newsfeeds that monitor the profession. For example, IFAC allows individuals to subscribe to receive news and updates from committees and the independent standard setting boards, as well as receiving electronic newsletters covering a variety of topical areas. See https://www.ifac.org/subscriptions for details (free account required). Other news aggregators, larger consulting and accounting firms, research companies, and specialty associations (such the Ethics & Compliance Initiative—see http://www.ethics.org) can also be used to enhance your environmental scanning.

Establish processes to scan for advancements in the CBAETC field. Best practices in CBAETC, as in every field, are constantly evolving. Watch for opportunities to enhance your organization's programs over time.

For example, some PAOs are investigating how to use technology to better enable the assessment of critical thinking skills. AICPA recently explored various ways to test written communication skills at a higher-order skill level and then to evaluate those abilities in a computerized scoring environment. They concluded, however, that the process of objectively evaluating a candidate's application of higher-order skills (thought process and judgment) within the context of a written response, is currently cost- and time-prohibitive. Accordingly, the AICPA has accelerated research into more advanced automated essay-scoring technology. Additionally, with the assistance of third-party testing experts, the AICPA is continuing to research potential alternatives to evaluating professional skepticism, which could result in developing new types of questions for the CPA Exam.[8]

Also, don't forget about the value of watching out for the education, training, and certification innovations occurring in other professions. It's easy to inadvertently become somewhat myopic on one's own profession, particular during large change projects, and miss best practices being developed by other professional organizations.

B6. Become an ambassador and mentor for CBAETC

The gains that your organization has made and the competence you have developed in implementing CBAETC are important to the professional community. Your organization's experience will be enhanced and solidified by helping other organizations that are just embarking on their own CBAETC journey. Sharing your expertise and collaborating with other organizations can be a valuable source of new partners to share resources and develop mutually beneficial program elements with.

Milestones of success

Congratulations! You have completed your initial CBAETC initiative! You have piloted or run an initial offering of new courses and may have implemented new accreditation partnerships. You have launched new requirements and have evaluated the initial results.

But your CBAETC journey is far from over—by now you will have realized that CBAETC strives for continuous improvement. Implementing CBAETC has developed skills and competence in your team that you will use going forward to continually evaluate and improve your processes and programs, to better equip current and future professional accountants to serve employers, clients and the public competently and effectively.

You are also now in the position to encourage others in your region to embark on their own CBAETC journey, and to assist and advise them based on your own experience, challenges and successes.

CONCLUSION

Too many PAO qualification programs remain focused on knowledge regurgitation and the mechanics of bookkeeping. Graduates of such programs have declining prospects of finding long-term employment in the increasingly digitized, global world in which technician-level work is fast becoming a commodity. Professional accountants are no longer being perceived as boring "bean counters," as clients and employers look progressively to them for higher-level skills—for example, in understanding the economics of transactions and events and then making judgments to ensure that financial information faithfully reflects the underlying economics and thereby provides more relevant inputs as a basis for informing resource allocation decisions. This is not to say that professional accountants can ignore journal entry preparation—understanding the fundamentals of the field will always unpin applications of professional judgment and because the judgments needed for non-routine transactions are significantly more difficult to automate. To remain relevant, however, professional accountants must predominantly provide the critical thinking, analysis, and evaluation skills that enable them to provide the value that organizations and clients—and ultimately the public—expects of professionals.

The transition to CBAETC, for both IPD and CPD, may be challenging for PAOs and universities, but they are able to draw on a wealth of existing experience and knowledge from other organizations around the world who have been or are proceeding through the process. When successfully implemented, CBAETC:

- Offers an up-to-date and comprehensive competency framework that serves as a core document for the profession (together with the code of ethics) and clearly identifies and describes the requisite competencies and specifies proficiency levels and knowledge topics for each domain and specialization
- Provides a detailed competency map documenting the links between the competency framework and formal education and practical experience
- Develops operational capacity with competent instructors using appropriate education materials and methods
- Promotes effective practical experience supervisors overseeing relevant workplace experience against a background of well-coordinated collaboration with PAOs, accounting academia (teaching and research), and professional accountants; and
- Enables the assurance of competent PAO members, certifying that members can apply their technical knowledge using high-order skills to make appropriate judgments in complex situations, and effectively communicate the relevant outputs of their work.

Ultimately, CBAETC provides the foundation for universities to prepare students for their careers and for PAOs to support their public interest mandate.

Examples of how CBAETC has been used in a variety of jurisdictions are presented in appendix A. Several of these examples have been referred to above. Review the additional examples to gain a fuller understanding of the broad applicability of CBAETC.

NOTES

1. World Bank Report on the Observance of Standards and Codes Accounting and Auditing http://web.worldbank.org/WBSITE/EXTERNAL/COUNTRIES/ECAEXT/EXTCENFI NREPREF/0,,contentMDK:21569478~menuPK:7356128~pagePK:64168445~piPK:64168309 ~theSitePK:4152118,00.html
2. Republic of Serbia ROSC A&A Update (June 2015): viii (see http://documents.worldbank .org/curated/en/557921479710152064/Serbia-Report-on-the-Observance-of-Standards -and-Codes-ROSC-on-accounting-and-auditing-update).
3. https://www.cpacanada.ca/en/become-a-cpa/pathways-to-becoming-a-cpa/national -education-resources/the-cpa-competency-map
4. https://www.saica.co.za/LearnersStudents/Examinations/Informationonwhatwill beexamined/CompetencyFramework/tabid/780/language/en-ZA/Default.asp
5. See The Pathways Commission: Charting a National Strategy for the Next Generation of Accountants (July 2012) Chapter 7_complete with detailed tables.pdf (290 KB) http:// commons.aaahq.org/posts/a3470e7ffa
6. The CFRR PULSAR webpage is http://web.worldbank.org/WBSITE/EXTERNAL /COUNTRIES/ECAEXT/EXTCENFINREPREF/0,,contentMDK:23762127~pagePK :64168445~piPK:64168309~theSitePK:4152118,00.html; the Competency Framework is available directly at: http://siteresources.worldbank.org/EXTCENFINREPREF/Resour ces/4152117-1509403435007/9950109-1531347933627/fincop10.pdf
7. Reprinted with permission from The University of Cape Town College of Accounting, Cape Town, South Africa. Any changes to the original material are the sole responsibility of the authors (and/or publisher) and have not been reviewed or endorsed by The University of Cape Town College of Accounting.
8. http://www.aicpa.org/BecomeACPA/CPAExam/nextexam/DownloadableDocuments /2016-practice-analysis-final-report.pdf

REFERENCES

Anderson, L. W. D. R. Krathwohl, B. S. Bloom. 2001. *A Taxonomy for Teaching, Learning, and Assessing: A Revision of Bloom's Taxonomy of Educational Objectives.* Complete Edition. New York: Longman.

Barth, M. E. 2008. Global Financial Reporting: Implications for U.S. Academics. *The Accounting Review* 83 (5): 1159–79.

IFAC (International Federation of Accountants). 2015. *Framework for International Education Standards for Professional Accountants and Aspiring Professional Accountants.* New York: IFAC.

Wells, M. J. C. 2011. Framework-Based Approach to Teaching Principle-Based Accounting Standards. *Accounting Education* 20 (4): 303–16.

A

Case Studies

APPENDIX A1. CASE STUDY—POLAND: IMPLEMENTATION OF CBAETC BY THE NATIONAL CHAMBER OF STATUTORY AUDITORS (KIBR)

Background and context

Poland's National Chamber of Statutory Auditors (KIBR) is responsible for regulating the country's statutory auditors. The process of auditor qualification is provided in figure A.1.

The prerequisite and Diploma Exams (DEs) are developed and offered under the authority of the Examination Commission, an independent body appointed by the Minister of Finance.

In 2016, Poland's Statutory Auditor profession was undergoing a period of significant challenges and change, fuelled by outdated systems, expanded globalization, competition from foreign PAOs, increased expectations from the EU and other international organizations, and a diminished ability to attract new members.

A World Bank project was undertaken to (1) to improve access to the profession in the context of the country's economic growth, while simultaneously (2) strengthening auditing and accounting education to meet the public's demand for competent auditors. The project focused on addressing the dual needs by developing resources to help KIBR and the Examination Commission improve professional education for professional accountants and auditors, as well as providing an approach to improve professional access. There were three main groups of resource deliverables:

1. Drafting the KIBR *Framework of Learning Outcomes* to assist with IES compliance
2. Re-developing the DE to be made up of longer, more integrated and more in-depth, competency-based business cases to evaluate the learning outcomes in the *Framework*; and

FIGURE A.1
General pathway of education, exams, and experience

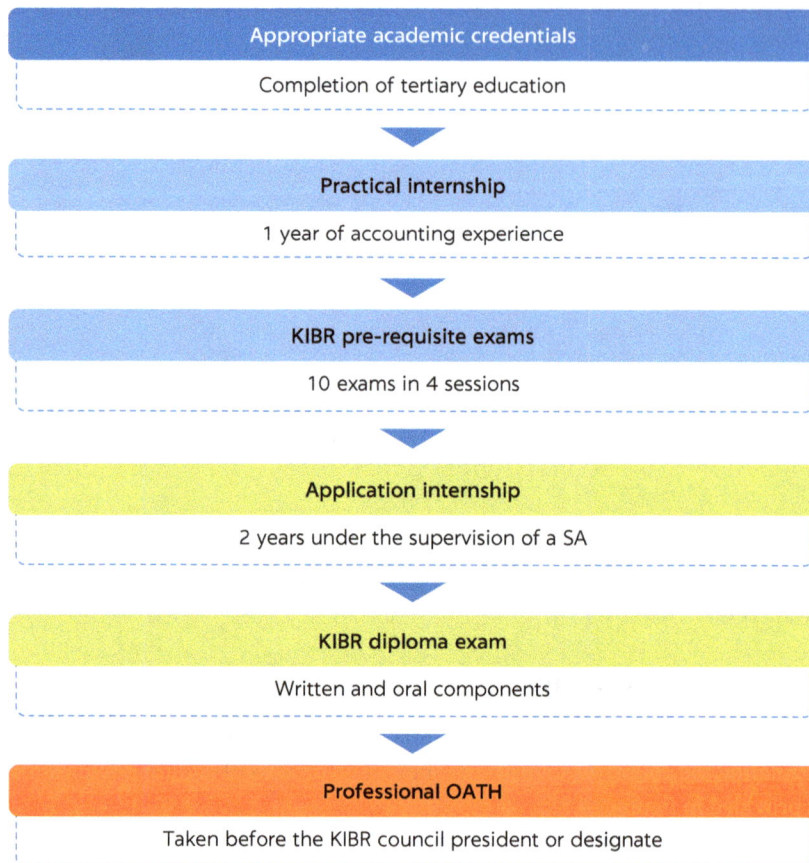

| Appropriate academic credentials |
| Completion of tertiary education |

| Practical internship |
| 1 year of accounting experience |

| KIBR pre-requisite exams |
| 10 exams in 4 sessions |

| Application internship |
| 2 years under the supervision of a SA |

| KIBR diploma exam |
| Written and oral components |

| Professional OATH |
| Taken before the KIBR council president or designate |

Source: www.WorldBank.org/CFRR.

3. Introducing a two-step process for accrediting universities and granting exemptions from the KIBR Pre-requisite Exams, using a model that reflects a strong and mutually beneficial partnership between the profession and the universities.

Implementing CBAETC

The extent to which CBAETC was implemented, and the methodology used is discussed below, using the structure of the CBAETC stages.

Stage 0: Evaluate readiness and resources

As described above, funding for the project came through the World Bank, as part of a comprehensive financial reporting reform project in Poland. As such, budgeting was performed by the World Bank team and the consulting firm performing the work assignment, as opposed to being compiled by KIBR. One of the first steps undertaken was to understand the authority structures in the country and the relationships between the Ministry of Finance, KIBR, and the Examination Commission. Because each group had shared responsibility and authority in the area of auditor education and certification, the project required direct involvement and collaboration between the groups.

With respect to evaluating the capability of local educators, the project team visited several prominent universities and interviewed key professors to evaluate levels of expertise and availability. Although levels of experience with competency-based education varied considerably between individuals, many professors in the country had been using competency-based approaches to one extent or another in their classrooms. This bode well for the ability for KIBR and the Examination Commission to make lasting change.

Stage 1: Establish the Competency Framework

Due to time and other resource constraints, KIBR opted to use a condensed approach to developing a competency framework. External consultants with significant experience in CBAETC used the IAESB's IESs as a starting point—with IFAC permissions—to develop what became called the *KIBR Framework of Learning Outcomes*. The term "learning outcomes" rather than "competencies" was chosen to reflect the fact that a full Practice Analysis had not been done. This was consistent with the IES language on which the Framework was largely based.

The Framework was initially developed with insight from a few key stakeholders, and then a workshop was held with representatives from relevant stakeholders, including KIBR, the Ministry of Finance, and the Examination Commission. Workshop participants had a broad range of background experience and perspectives, including public practice, professional education and university academia. One of the key developments from this broader stakeholder involvement was that several proficiency levels were increased from the base level in the IESs, due to KIBR's focus on certifying audit professionals, rather than general professional accountants. After revising the draft statements and proficiency levels based on workshop feedback, the resulting *Framework of Learning Outcomes* served as the core for future project activities.

The first draft knowledge topic lists were the required lists of theoretical knowledge for the pre-requisite exams, which were codified directly in regulations.

Stage 2: Evaluate the current program to determine gaps

In evaluating the current program, the knowledge topic lists were mapped to the learning outcomes, which allowed for an evaluation of where the learning outcomes were not currently covered in the exams and syllabi. The main gaps in coverage were in some of the breadth areas of governance, risk management and internal control; strategy and management; organizational environment; and information technology; as well as in the enabling areas of professional skills, values, ethics, and attitudes. KIBR planned to address these gaps in future, working with the relevant Ministries as necessary to adapt regulation.

Other elements of the current program were not made available to be mapped during the program, due to sensitivities around exam security, and the scope of the immediate project. Local stakeholders were left with recommendations and instructions for completing this mapping.

Stage 3: Develop an expanded program

The project scope was limited to developing a new competency-based Diploma Examination for certification, and developing an accreditation program for university courses. Both of these elements drew heavily on the *Framework of Learning Outcomes*. The DE was fully referenced to the Framework and was designed from the outset to deliver adequate coverage of the Framework over a reasonable period of time. This was specified on the exam design documents

TABLE A.1 **Resources required**

RESOURCES REQUIRED (ALL FIGURES ARE APPROXIMATE):	
Consulting days (90% foreign experts, 10% local consultants)	160
In-country days for foreign experts (requiring hotels, meals, etc.)	110
Group meeting and event days (requiring meeting venues, transportation, and/or accommodation and meals for participants)	12
Hours of simultaneous translation	40
Pages translated	450

Source: World Bank CFRR.

(Blueprint and other design specifications). Exam cases were built to test specific learning outcomes at the required levels, and comprehensive scoring guidance was developed to ensure reliability and consistency during the scoring process, using graduated performance grids that described the expected methods of demonstrating competence.

The university accreditation model was developed to allow students of accredited universities to receive exam exemptions from KIBR on successful completion of specific university courses. The model requires that accredited universities support the development of competence in students by adhering to best practices, such as actively engaging students through collaboration and learner-centric approaches. At the knowledge topic level, university courses were required to demonstrate adequate coverage of the required topics in their courses before receiving exemption status for courses.

Stage 4: Implement the expanded program

KIBR is currently working on the implementation stage for project elements. It was known by KIBR from the outset that a great deal of collaboration would be needed between stakeholders and that implementation would be a slow process. The project's outputs are currently being used to facilitate these collaborative efforts and move towards implementation.

This condensed approach to partially implementing CBAETC took place over approximately 12 months.

Additionally, resources were provided by the World Bank CFRR, KiBR and the Ministry of Finance in terms of oversight and review, meeting venues and administrative support (table A.1).

APPENDIX A2. CASE STUDY—SERBIA: PROJECT FOR IMPROVING ACCOUNTING AND AUDIT CURRICULA FOR UNIVERSITY AND PROFESSIONAL EDUCATION PROGRAMS

Background and context

In Serbia, the Chamber of Auditors enjoys statutory recognition, and the Chamber's membership is mandatory for licensed auditors and all audit firms. The Audit Law (2013) gives the Chamber, among other things, the mandate to:

- Prepare the program of qualifying examination for certified auditors, organize qualifying examinations for certified auditors and issue certificates to statutory auditors
- Prepare a continuing professional education program and organize continuing professional education of licensed certified auditors.

The Serbian Association of Accountants and Auditors (SAAA) is a voluntary membership organization for both accountants and auditors in Serbia. It was founded in 1955 and has been a full member of the International Federation of Accountants® (IFAC) since 1997. The SAAA education program is based on the education program of the Association of Chartered Certified Accountants (ACCA).

The leading four Public Universities in Serbia which offer Degree Programs with a concentration in accounting and audit are:

- University of Belgrade
- University of Novi Sad
- University of Nis
- University of Kragujevac.

The Report on the Observance of Standards and Codes on Accounting and Auditing (ROSC) for the Republic of Serbia, published in June 2015, identified some weaknesses in the university accounting curriculum, especially related to international accounting and auditing standards. It also identified that accounting education tends to focus on rules, and needs to move towards competency-based programs. Furthermore, it identified the need to establish stronger links between university-level programs and professional audit training programs.

Implementing STAR-CFR

In the aftermath of the publication of the ROSC, a Euro 3.4 million grant was given by the Government of Switzerland for the "Serbia Technical Assistance for Reform of Corporate Financial Reporting" (STAR-CFR). The project was launched in June 2016, and the project end date was set for December 2019.

The project had several components, some of which were to be implemented by the Ministry of Finance of the Republic of Serbia ("recipient-executed components"), whereas other components were to be implemented by the World Bank's Centre for Financial Reporting Reform (CFRR), based in Vienna, Austria ("Bank-executed components").

The recipient-executed components included a budget of Euro 1 million dedicated to training a large audience comprising regulators, preparers and auditors of financial statements in the public and private sectors, as well as university lecturers and other trainers in the use and application of IFRS® Standards, International Standards on Auditing (ISA), and other financial reporting issues.

Improved knowledge of international standards amongst the academic community is a key requirement for accounting education reforms to be viable.

The Bank-executed components were dedicated to supporting accounting education in the following four thematic areas:

- Assessment and possible improvement of the accountancy curriculum in the university sector
- Assessment and possible improvement of professional education programs through the Chamber of Auditors and other competent professional accountancy organizations (PAOs), including pre-qualification education, training, examinations, seminars and workshops

- Provision of assessments, toolkits, and other support for Continuing Professional Development (CPD) programs
- Assistance in implementing improved tools in training programs, and support for training programs for accountants and auditors.

The project was in progress at the time of writing of this Guide, and the World Bank project team had laid out the following activities to achieve the required changes:

1. Benchmarking Study
2. Practice Analysis
3. Revised Curriculum
4. Capacity-building Activities.

The project activities are described briefly below, in the context of the CBAETC journey stages.

Stage 0: Evaluate readiness and resources

Although the 2015 ROSC described weaknesses in the university curricula in Serbia, the World Bank team also noted some significant capabilities in the universities and PAOs being worked with. For example, several university professors had prior experience developing their own case-based questions, and the PAOs had made advancements in examinations that moved towards a more learning outcomes approach. Lacking were sufficient internal financial resources, specific expertise, and capacity to implement CBAETC in a broader and deeper manner without some external assistance.

As described above, a grant was given by the Government of Switzerland for the "Serbia Technical Assistance for Reform of Corporate Financial Reporting" (STAR-CFR). Activities for implementing CBAETC are included within the Bank-executed components, and are allocated funds from the overall STAR-CFR budget. This allowed sufficient financial support to undertake the previously discussed goals and themes.

Stage 1: Establish the Competency Framework and Stage 2: Evaluate the current program to determine gaps

A benchmarking study and modified practice analysis were launched in parallel to:

- Determine the full range of competencies essential for professional accountants and auditors and assess their importance from various key stakeholder perspectives, and
- Evaluate the gaps between the existing situation and the desired state.

Practice Analysis

In parallel with the benchmarking study, a practice analysis was launched. Based on resource availability and cost/benefit factors, a condensed approach was used to perform a modified practice analysis. The analysis was conducted through interviews of 46 representatives of various stakeholders, which represented PAOs, academia, private local companies, multinationals, state-owned enterprises, as well as accounting and audit companies. These stakeholders provided valuable insight as to the relative importance of technical and non-technical competencies for accountants and auditors in the Serbian context.

Benchmarking study

The Accounting Degree Programs of the four Public Universities identified above, as well as the professional qualification (PQ) programs of the Chamber of Auditors and the SAAA were assessed using the benchmarking tool developed by the CFRR (see www.worldbank.org/cfrr). The benchmarking tool incorporates learning outcomes of the ACCA and the Chartered Institute of Public Finance and Accountancy (CIPFA) Programs, which are grouped into four different areas:

- Management and management accounting
- Financial accounting and reporting
- Audit and assurance
- Financial management.

Conducting this analysis helps identify areas of teaching which may need particular attention, but it also results in immediate improvements as Faculty members are able in some cases to remedy quite easily some of the learning gaps identified. It also assists Universities to achieve exemptions for graduating students into some internationally recognized professional accountancy education programs. Finally, it helps build the commitment of Faculty members and PAO trainers to the reform program.

Stage 3: Develop an expanded program and Stage 4: Implement the expanded program

Revised curriculum

The benchmarking study and the practice analysis led to a common set of recommendations on revising the content of University Degree Programs with a concentration in accounting and audit, as well as Professional Certification Programs:

- Several technical competencies need to be introduced into these programs
- Non-technical skills and competencies also need to be introduced so that graduates and young professionals acquire in particular:
  - Experience with practical tools such as EXCEL and accounting software
  - Skills such as communication, ethics, and professional judgment.

These additional skills and competencies were presented to representatives of Universities and PAOs in a 2-day workshop.

Capacity building activities

Having reached a consensus on the changes required in accounting education, a number of capacity-building workshops have been scheduled to assist Universities and PAOs implement these changes.

- The "recipient-executed" component of the project will provide the technical knowledge required to ensure all course materials and training programs are aligned with the latest international accounting and auditing standards
- The "Bank-executed" component of the project will focus on developing the capacity of educators to implement competency-based education.

A series of workshops are being scheduled under the "Bank-executed" component and will address a range of themes, including:

- Turning learning outcomes into competency-based education programs
- Constructive alignment between learning outcomes, instruction methods, and assessment of competencies

- Integrative courses and examinations, which is one of the key features of a professional certification program
- Continuing Professional Development: How to develop and implement a competency-based CPD Program for practicing accountants and auditors in compliance with good international practices.

In order to be most effective, the following practices were adopted throughout this capacity-building phase of the project:

- Offer tailored assistance when required: To complement the large workshops aimed at achieving cost efficiencies, customized workshops are being implemented to assist PAO and individual Universities address their unique circumstances and requirements
- Deliver practical, "competency-based" workshops: This helps trainers implement immediate changes in their programs by working on practical examples and cases
- Develop sample materials and tools that trainers will be able to adapt and use in their ongoing efforts to improve their programs, beyond the limited time frame of the project.

APPENDIX A3. CASE STUDY—SOUTH AFRICA: IMPLEMENTATION OF CBAETC IN CONJUNCTION WITH FRAMEWORK-BASED TEACHING

A good practice example is found in South Africa where extensive research, development and consultation over a 3-year period (2007–09) resulted in a "revolutionary" new CA(SA) 2010 training program centered on a new Competency Framework. This appendix highlights aspects of the project that relate primarily to Stage 3: Design and Develop an Expanded Program. The South African Institute of Chartered Accountants (SAICA) supported its move to CBAETC by developing detailed guidance for the successful completion of two phases of formal education and a practical experience component that constitute IPD.

Note that some documents referenced below have been updated and revised to take account of subsequent developments.

SAICA's guidance regarding competencies assessed in program elements include:

- Detailed Guidance for the Academic Program (2014): https://www.saica.co .za/Portals/0/LearnersStudents/documents/Detailed_Guidance_to_the _competency_framework_for_the_academic_programme_Updated_and _approved_July_2014.pdf
- CA(SA) Training Programmed: Prescribed Competencies (effective 1 January 2010; latest revision 2015): https://www.saica.co.za/Portals/0/Trainees /documents/SAICA_Training_Programme_Competencies_2016.pdf
- Training Programmed: Implementation Guide (January 2016): https://www .saica.co.za/trainees/training/theca2010trainingprogramme/tabid/1657 /language/en-US/default.aspx
- A range of up-to-date assessment resources, assessment instruments and generic training plans to support SAICA Training Programmed practical experience supervisors to execute their roles effectively: https://www.saica .co.za/Training/Training/AssessmentofTrainees/tabid/420/language /en-ZA/Default.aspx.

Universities accredited by SAICA to provide the formal education components that are prerequisites to registering for SAICA's Initial Test of Competence (ITC) and Assessment of Professional Competence (APC) evaluations adapted their teaching materials and methods to develop the relevant competencies in their students. Good practice examples include the financial reporting staff of the University of Cape Town's College of Accounting who gave effect to the financial reporting aspects of SAICA's detailed guidance on the academic program by:

- Redesigning their financial reporting courses ensuring well considered topic allocations and scaffolding from one course to the next
- Adopting a framework-based teaching approach and embedding it in all of the College's financial reporting courses
- Delivering training in framework-based teaching to their tutors; and
- Developing framework-based teaching materials and, through the LearnAccounting website, sharing these materials with others (available at http://learnaccounting.uct.ac.za—free account required).

APPENDIX A4. CASE STUDY—THE PHILIPPINES: RE-DESIGNING THE ACCOUNTANCY CURRICULUM

Background and context

The accountancy profession in the Philippines is regulated by the Professional Regulatory Board of Accountancy (BoA). The country's recognized Professional Accountancy Organization is the Philippine Institute of Certified Public Accountants (PICPA). There are more than 188,000 Certified Public Accountants (CPAs) registered in the Philippines, of which over 8,000 are currently active CPAs in Public Practice.

To practice accountancy in the Philippines, the requirements are:

1. The completion of a Bachelor of Science in Accountancy (BSA) from a University accredited by the Commission on Higher Education (CHED), and
2. Successful completion of the CPA Licensure examination.

Recently, the CHED and the BoA approved three new university accounting programs in addition to the reformatted BSA.

Work experience can be gained in any of the four recognized areas (Public Practice, Commerce and Industry, Academia and Education, and Government). For CPAs in Public Practice, a 3-year meaningful experience must be completed. In addition, accreditation must be achieved from a range of different regulatory bodies depending on the industry and other characteristics of their clients.

The existing CPA Licensure examination in the Philippines is usually taken shortly after completion of a BSA and is administered exclusively through a six-paper multiple-choice examination. The existing licensure examinations for CPAs covers the following subjects:

- Taxation and Regulatory Framework for Business Transactions
- Financial Accounting and Reporting
- Advanced Financial Accounting and Reporting
- Auditing
- Management Advisory Services.

A number of factors led the different stakeholders involved in the certification and regulation of the accounting profession to recognize the need to re-design the accountancy curriculum. These factors included:

- The need to achieve greater compliance with International Education Standards (IESs) which had been significantly modified in the past 10 years
- The need to ensure different specializations for accountants were recognized, whereas the existing education and certification model favored the public practice stream to the detriment of other areas of practice
- The opportunity to achieve greater regional mobility for members of the profession in particular through the Mutual Recognition Agreements (MRAs) for professional services under the ASEAN Economic Community (AEC) established in 2015
- The implementation of the "K to 12 Program" which added two additional years of studies in the high school level in order to provide sufficient time for mastery of concepts and skills, develop lifelong learners, and prepare high school graduates for tertiary education, employment, and entrepreneurship.

Stage 0: Evaluate readiness and resources

The key stakeholders in this project were the Professional Regulatory the BoA and the CHED.

- The BoA is one of the 43 Boards established under the authority of the Professional Regulatory Commission (PRC). The PRC is the national government agency mandated to enforce laws regulating the various professions. The Boards govern their respective professions' practice and ethical standards, and accredit the professional organization representing the professionals. The BoA consists of a Chairman and six members appointed by the President of the Philippines, based an initial list of 5 nominees prepared by PICPA, from which the PRC will make 3 recommendations for appointment
- CHED was created under the Higher Education Act of 1994, and its responsibilities include setting minimum standards for programs and institutes of higher education as well as imposing sanctions for poor performance. In addition to regulating higher education, CHED is also responsible for developing policies to support quality improvement in the higher educational system.

As noted in the World Bank's Report on the Observance of Standards and Codes on Accounting and Auditing for the Republic of the Philippines, published in June 2017, PICPA does not have adequate resources to fully discharge its various roles, let alone commit the resources required to support the overhaul of the qualifications for professional accountants and auditors. Furthermore, it does not have the mandate to administer professional certification examinations, as exam administration is under the purview of the BoA.

Whilst CHED has the mandate and resources to develop and implement revised undergraduate degree programs at Universities, and the BoA has the mandate and resources to adopt a revised curriculum for the subjects covered by the CPA Licensure Examination(s), they will be seeking external support and resources to ensure the reforms are conducted in an effective manner. Volunteering, cooperation, and leveraging resources available through regional and global networks will also be key to the success of this project.

Stage 1: Establish the Competency Framework

CHED adopted an outcomes-based approach to education and published a Handbook on typology, outcomes-based education, and institutional sustainability assessment was published by CHED in 2014.

The Philippine Accountancy Education Framework (PAEF) provides the minimum standards and requirements for the accountancy degree programs that can be offered by the higher education institutions. It encompasses academic degrees, initial and CPD, as well as the professional certifications and qualifications.

The PAEF was revised and became consistent with the latest competency framework for professional accountants issued by the IFAC through its IESs, including IES 2 (Technical Competence), IES 3 (Professional Skills), and IES 4 (Professional values, ethics and attitudes). In other words, it relied on the Learning Outcomes of the IESs to define its competencies, rather than running a full Practice Analysis. The PAEF uses a learner-centered and outcome-based approach that is geared towards addressing the requirements of the profession and users of its services (figure A.2).

Stage 2: Evaluate the current program to determine gaps

A significant amount of research was undertaken by the different stakeholders involved in the training and certification of accountants and auditors in the Philippines. Discussions and information gathering was conducted through a range of global and regional organizations, some of the which the Philippines is actively engaged in. These included the IFAC, the ASEAN Federation of Accountants (AFA), and the Confederation of Asian and Pacific Accountants (CAPA).

FIGURE A.2

Philippine Accounting Education Framework

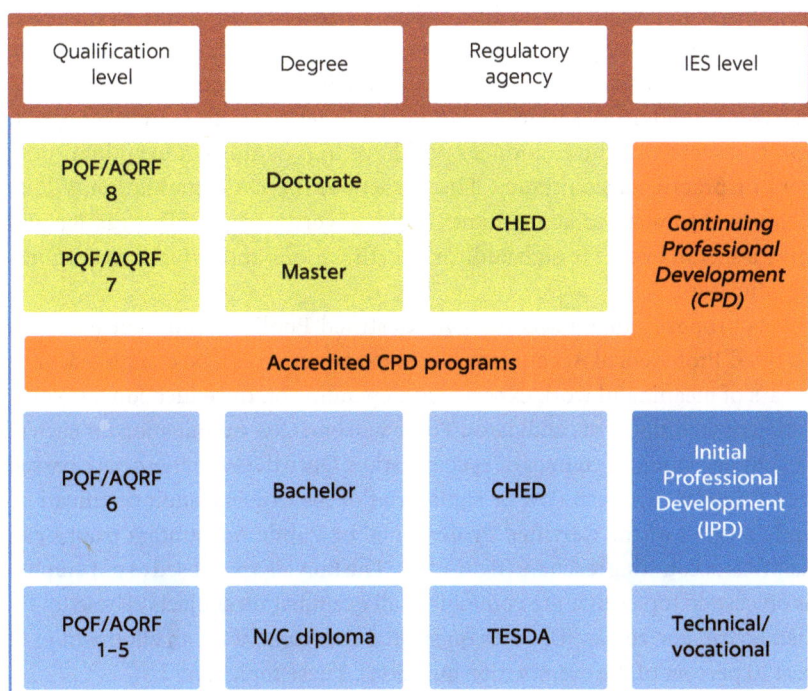

Source: Adapted from World Bank 2017.
Note: AQRF = ASEAN Qualifications Reference Framework; CHED = Commission on Higher Education; CPD = Continuing Professional Development; IES: International Education Standards; PQF = Philippine Qualification Framework; TESDA: Technical Education and Skills Development Authority (Philippines).

Some of the factors and trends leading to the revised curriculum included the need for harmonization and integration with:

- The Philippine Qualification Framework (PQF)
- The ASEAN Qualifications Reference Framework (AQRF)
- Internationally recognized foreign qualifications (to facilitate MRAs)
- The requirements of industry (to strengthen certain competencies of CPAs entering the job market).

A review of the global trends led to the conclusion that "one size does not fit all" and accountancy qualifications need to reflect the growing specialization of the accounting industry.

In June 2015, the BoA revised the subjects covered by the CPA Licensure Examination to the set presently in place.

Stage 3: Design and develop an expanded program

After a series of consultations which included a series of public meetings around the country, four different yet related accounting programs at the bachelor level were established. These are:

- The revised BS in Accountancy (BSA) for the CPA track
- BS in Management Accounting (BSMA) for the management accounting track
- BS in Internal Audit (BSIA) for the governance, risk, and compliance track, and
- BS in Accounting Information Systems (BSAIS) for the information and technology track.

In addition to these changes in the accountancy education at the University level, it is also envisioned that there will also be a reformatting of the professional licensure examination process. The licensure examination of the future will include two levels of tests. The graduates of the four accounting programs will have to take the first-level Certified Accountant (CA) examination. This examination consists of five core accounting subjects, to include financial accounting reporting, advanced financial accounting reporting, management advisory services, taxation and regulatory framework for business transactions. The examinees will have to pass this CA examination to work or practice accountancy. The passers of the CA examination will be authorized to work as accountants in the government, public practice and private sector, except to sign auditor's certifications and to teach as accounting educators.

It is proposed that a second-level Certified Public Accountant (CPA) or Certified Professional Accountant (CPA) examination can be completed, after 3 years of meaningful work experience, depending on the educational specialization or attainment of candidates. There will be a CPA examination for each of the four accountancy courses or specialization. Once the examinees have passed the CPA exam, they can now be signatories of the external audit certification, while passers of the Certified Professional or Public Accountant exams can qualify as accounting teachers (figure A.3). The BoA also proposed to put emphasis on certain topics that are common to all examination subjects. These topics shall be categorized as "Updates on special concerns" with an allotment of at least 10 percent of the examination questions. These topics are:

1. Globalization trends
2. Digital information technology trends

3. Governance and ethics
4. Regulatory requirements and considerations
5. Effective business communication.

Stage 4: Implement the expanded program

The Policies, standards, and guidelines for the four undergraduate degree programs were published as CHED Memorandum Orders 27–30 in March 2017.

The Memorandum Orders are comprehensive and adopt an outcomes-based approach. They include a detailed study program, provide detailed guidelines on the means of curriculum delivery, and mandate internship and research requirements. The prescribed competencies in the revised IESs provide a foundation to the curriculum for the four accounting programs. A capstone examination requirement is to be included in the revised curriculum, at least 400 hours practicum with research to address practical experience as part of graduates' Initial Professional Development, as well as a professional designation tied to each specialty.

The orders also provide guidelines on the resources required and address availability of a library, laboratory, and other physical facilities. The qualifications and teaching load of Faculty members, as well as CPD requirements for Faculty and other Staff are also addressed. The Memorandum Orders also provide a benchmark for CHED's ongoing monitoring and evaluation of Higher Education Institutions.

The four specialized accounting programs are to be offered starting with the 2018/19 School Year.

The proposed licensure examinations consisting of both the CA and CPA examinations are anticipated to start by year 2023.

FIGURE A.3

Philippine Accountancy Education Framework (PAEF)

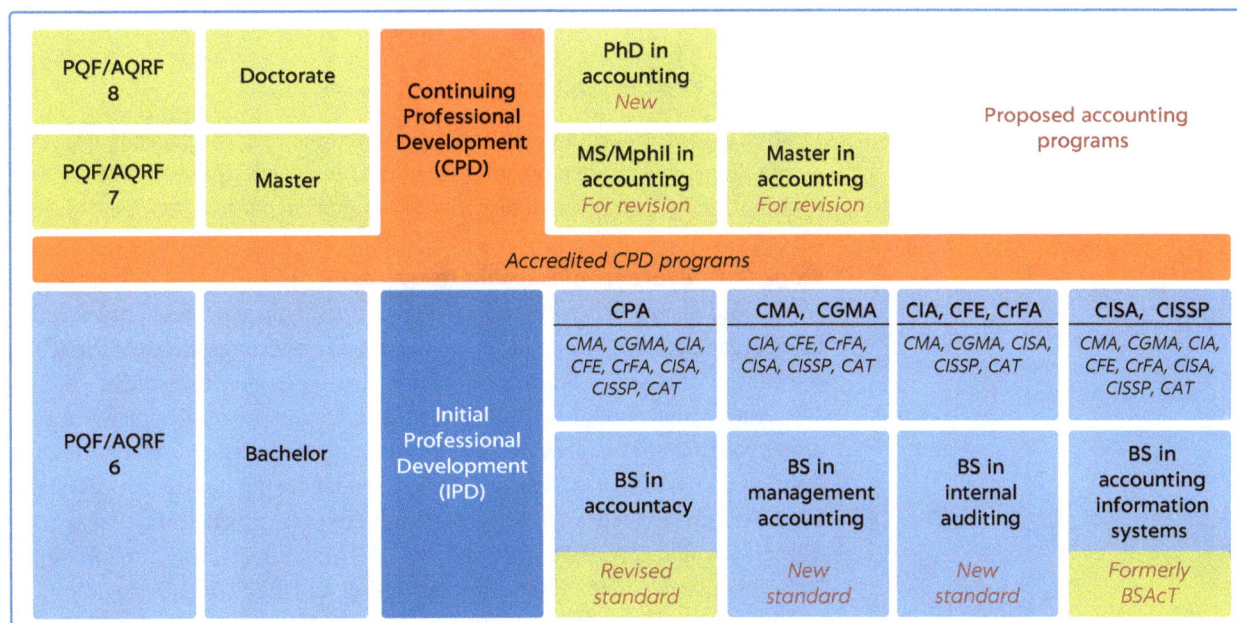

Source: World Bank 2017.

Note: AQRF = ASEAN Qualifications Reference Framework; BS = Bachelor of Science; CAT = Certified Accounting Technician; CFE = Certified Fraud Examiner; CRFA = Certified Retirement Financial Adviser; CGMA = Chartered Global Management Accountant; CHED = Commission on Higher Education; CIA = Certified Internal Auditor; CISA = Certified Information Systems Auditors; CISSP = Certified Information Systems Security Professional; CMA = Certified Management Accountant; CPD = Continuing Professional Development; PAEF = Philippines Accounting Education Framework; PQF = Philippine Qualification Framework.

APPENDIX A5. CASE STUDY—GHANA: REFORM OF THE CA QUALIFICATION THROUGH TWINNING WITH ICAEW

Background and context

The Institute of Chartered Accountants of Ghana (ICAG) is the sole regulator of the accountancy profession in the country. Established by the Chartered Accountants Act (1963), ICAG is a self-regulatory body governed by a Council of 11 chartered accountants, of which 4 are appointed by the Minister of Education, while the members of ICAG elect the remainder.

ICAG acts as both an examining body for awarding CA certification and the licensing authority for members engaged in public auditing practice. Its members are recognized under the Companies Code as sole auditors of company accounts. ICAG is a member of the IFAC and the Association of Accountancy Bodies in West Africa (ABWA).

The World Bank's *Report on the Observance of Standards and Codes on Accounting and Auditing* (ROSC-A&A) for Ghana, published in 2004, noted that there was a shortage of qualified accounting professionals in Ghana. ICAG membership stood at just over 1,000, with less than 4 percent female members, and only 109 members in public practice. Professionals with foreign accountancy qualifications held 48 percent of the total membership. At the time, there were more than 124,000 registered companies in Ghana.

As a result of the shortage, many companies were employing nonqualified persons in accounting positions, which was negatively affecting the quality of financial reporting.

The ROSC A&A report also noted that professional education and training were not adequate. Although ICAG's main entry requirement to the profession were in line with IFAC requirements, in practice, lower entry requirements were accepted. The ICAG-prescribed curriculum for educating and training of professional accountants was over a decade old. A proposed revised curriculum was set to become effective May 2005, however, it would still not fully meet the IFAC International Education Standards.

Key ROSC recommendations included the need to:

- Strengthen the accountancy profession by enhancing the capacity of ICAG, enabling it to operate more effectively and in line with the IFAC SMOs
- Enhance the quality and international recognition of the ICAG PQ.

Stage 0: Evaluate readiness and resources

ICAG needed strengthening to function effectively as a professional accountancy organization. The challenge included the financial resources of the ICAG secretariat, which were limited, contributing to operational difficulties.

Capacity gaps also included the ICAG certification program, which was outdated. Assistance was provided by the Institute of Chartered Accountants in England and Wales (ICAEW). A "twinning" relationship between ICAEW and ICAG was established, and World Bank funding was provided starting in 2011. Through twinning, ICAEW worked with ICAG to simultaneously develop capacity in governance, standards and administration, and the ICAG PQ program.

In 2015–16, a new ICAEW project was funded by the Department for International Development of the United Kingdom (DFID) and overseen by the IFAC. This was followed by a second phase (2016–17) and third phase (2017–18) of capacity building.

FIGURE A.4
Eight key dimensions of professional qualification

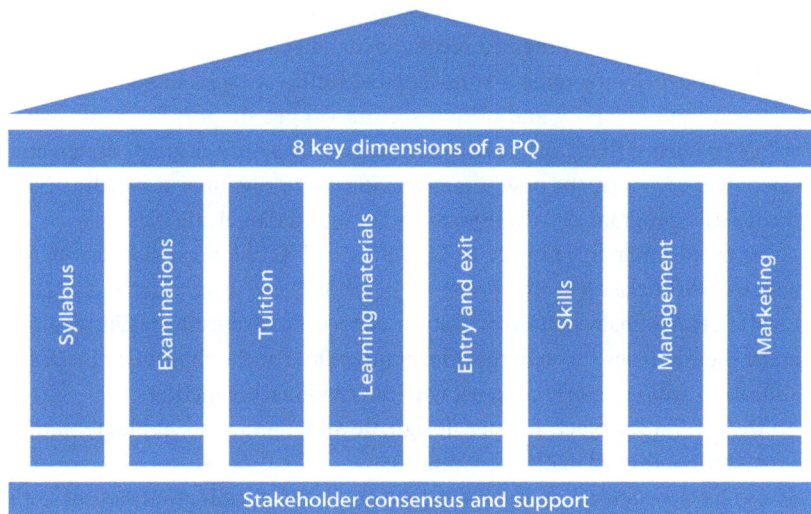

8 key dimensions of a PQ

Syllabus | Examinations | Tuition | Learning materials | Entry and exit | Skills | Management | Marketing

Stakeholder consensus and support

Source: Institute of Chartered Accountants in England and Wales (ICAEW) Capacity Building team. Used with permission; further permission required for reuse.

Under these projects, ICAEW was tasked with assisting ICAG in enhancing its professional accountancy qualification examination system. ICAEW would also develop roadmaps to enhancing accreditation of educational institutions and training offices, and the practical training and experience of newly qualified professional accountants. Project work was founded on the ICAEW 'Eight Pillars of an Effective Professional Qualification (PQ)' model to identify new interventions that would deliver immediate benefits (figure A.4).

Stage 1: Establish the Competency Framework

One of the key benefits of a twinning arrangement with a well-established PAO is the ability to draw on the mature PAO's existing systems and programs. As a result, ICAG was able to rely heavily on the Competency Framework that underpins the ICAEW's own program. Local consultation by the project team was used to make adjustments as appropriate.

The project set out to strengthen the ICAG profile and influence and its capacity to fully support Ghana's continued economic development. One of the outcomes of local consultations was the decision to include public sector accounting and finance in the syllabus of the professional examinations. This would support the implementation of IPSAS in the Public Sector.

Also, the technician qualification, which is regionally recognized and allows progression to the professional stage, was deemed important to maintain and strengthen as part of the program.

Stage 2: Evaluate the current program to determine gaps

At the beginning of the project, there were significant gaps in the ICAG program, as compared with the ICAEW program and other international benchmarks. The syllabus had not been reformed for 5 years, there were no learning materials of any quality, examinations were poorly weighted to the syllabus and instruction was very weak. Reflecting this, the big audit firms and other key employers were unhappy with ICAG performance.

Stage 3: Design and develop an expanded program and
Stage 4: Implement the expanded program

Over a number of years, ICAEW worked with ICAG to greatly improve the situation. The 2011–12 project prepared recommendations on revisions to the syllabus and held a series of joint seminars/workshops with different audiences—examiners, employers, the university and tuition sectors—to get support for launch of a new PQ. To ensure that gaps had been satisfactorily closed through design and development activities, the new Ghana qualification program was benchmarked to the ICAEW program, IFAC's IESs and other international qualifications.

As an extension to this project, ICAEW provided technical assistance to ICAG to acquire world class learning materials in 2013. These were a 'game changer'. Students of ICAG finally had all of the study materials and question banks required to assist their journey through the 3-level program. For the first time, the ICAG qualification could properly compete with international competitors.

In the 2015–18 project, further design, development, and implementation efforts were conducted in different phases:

Phase 1 work focused on improving the quality of examination setting at all 3 levels of the PQ. A program of workshops for examiners highlighted the benchmarks for quality in examination setting and got examiners to contribute questions that met the new quality criteria expected for Ghana. This phase also improved the examination processes and involved mentoring those at ICAG involved in this area. It also identified critical areas to focus on in the next two phases.

Phase 2 work focused on improving the quality of tuition and practical work experience (skills). A registration and grading scheme was launched for all tuition providers, with a view to grading (accrediting) all providers according to the quality criteria of their training establishments. Considerable support and mentoring was provided to the single largest tuition provider with over 1,000 students, the ICAG College. At the same time, an authorized training employer (ATE) scheme was launched for employers to join, so to bring practical work training under a common scheme that could be monitored closely. ICAEW also delivered a CPD program focusing on IFRS and IAS especially for the benefit of newly qualified accountants.

Phase 3 work focused on a complete refresh/reform of ICAG syllabus from 2012 as well as yet further strengthening of examination setting, the tuition provider grading scheme, the ICAG College and the ATE scheme. The additional workshops for ICAG examiners, moderators and markers was considered to be highly effective. There was also a detailed program of train-the-trainer courses that, in combination with support to the ICAG College and the tuition provider grading scheme, has much improved the quality of tuition.

Each phase of work has built on the achievements of the previous phase and overall there is good evidence of the benefits. Student registrations and membership over the period of interventions show substantial growth. This strongly suggests that the key overall goal for the project—increasing the number of professional accountants in Ghana—is happening.

The economy of Ghana across all sectors will benefit from further increases in qualified ICAG accountants and the associated pool of accountancy skills and services. By logical deduction, increased student numbers combined with increased pass rates will increase ICAG membership and improve the ratio of ICAG professional accountants to the Ghana population.

Stakeholders agree that the recent improvements to the examinations and tuition will result in higher pass rates. Therefore, ICAEW now recommends continued focus on pass rates, while still maintaining high quality examinations

Institute of Chartered Accountants of Ghana (ICAG) members and students

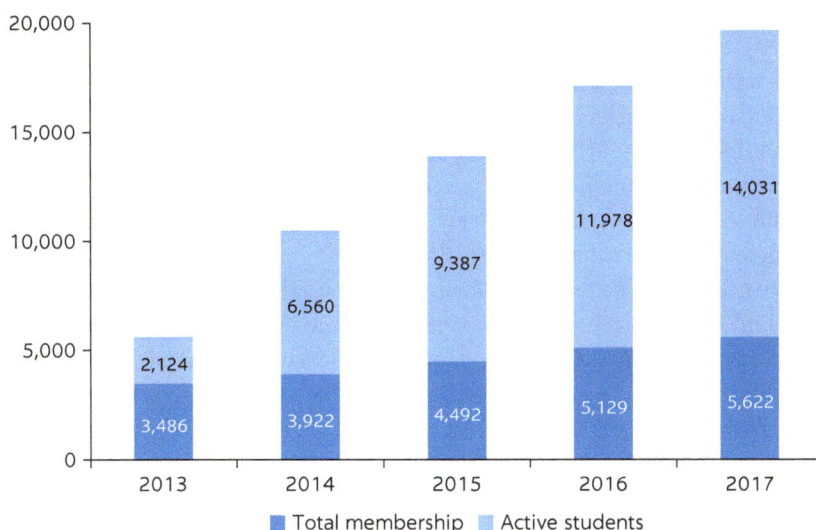

Source: Institute of Chartered Accountants in England and Wales (ICAEW) International Capacity Building team.

at an appropriate level of competence, as the most direct way to increase the number of ICAG professional accountants. (figure A.5)

In ICAEW, the conversion of students to professionals exceeds 80 percent while in ICAG the equivalent is less than 30 percent. This represents a loss of potential accountancy skills for ICAG and the Ghana economy. This challenge is also an opportunity to further strengthen Ghana's accountancy capacity in 2019 and beyond.

APPENDIX A6. PALESTINIAN WOMEN ACCOUNTING TECHNICIAN PROGRAM

Background and context

The level of unemployment in Palestine remains stubbornly high at 29 percent. The unemployment rate is especially high in Gaza in general (44 percent), and particularly affects the young, at 60 percent for those aged between 15 and 29.[1]

The World Bank's research highlighted a continuing mismatch between workforce skills and market needs in Palestine. Leading Palestinian private sector employers identified this mismatch as one of the principal reasons constraining their absorption of new labor market entrants into employment. During these discussions, the private sector stressed that this constraint is not limited to technical competence, but also includes a lack of critical soft skills needed to make young job seekers effective in jobs. Unemployment amongst young University graduates exceeds 50 percent.

The Palestinian Women Accounting Technicians (PWAT) program was a one-time program designed to provide a group of marginalized Palestinian women with basic accounting training which could lead to employment outcomes in a relatively short time frame.

Although this program was based on the technician level rather than the professional level, a competency-based approach was undertaken. As such, it provides a valuable illustration of CBAETC concepts as applied to technician programs.

Stage 0: Evaluate readiness and resources

The PWAT program was the collaborative effort of AMIDEAST, the World Bank, the Ministry of Women's Affairs and the Palestinian Association of Certified Public Accountants (PACPA). Sufficient funding was available to run a program for 72 women.

Ensuring the competence of the trainers in the program was achieved by setting detailed and demanding selection criteria and advertising the trainer positions broadly. Prospective trainers for technical content submitted CVs for review and were interviewed by a panel of representatives from AMIDEAST and PACPA. A total of 14 qualified trainers submitted applications, and the 3 most competent candidates were hired. Soft-skills trainers were chosen based on prior work performed for the collaborating organizations.

To maximize success, women were chosen to participate in the program based on demonstrated interest and apparent capacity to undertake and benefit from the program. The selection criteria for admission into the program included the following:

- Being unemployed
- Demonstrating openness to new education and career opportunities
- Having a clear commitment to the program
- Completion of formal secondary education.

The criteria related to openness and commitment were considered particularly important, given that the program was offered free of charge (payment of student fees usually demonstrates and secures student interest and commitment, but these indicators could not be relied upon for this project).

Completion of formal secondary education was also a fundamental requirement, as the program was to be delivered over a few weeks, which meant there would be no opportunity for students to brush up on basic skills that would be required to successfully complete the program.

Preference was given to younger women who were just starting their careers, especially those who had at least some exposure to the workplace and basic business concepts. Interestingly, half of the students ultimately selected for the program had completed an undergraduate degree, although the majority were from Open Universities which tend to have a low employment rate and target socio-economically disadvantaged women.

Stage 1: Establish the Competency Framework;
Stage 2: Evaluate the current program to determine gaps

The PWAT program did not use a specific Competency Framework. Nonetheless, the program curriculum was developed based on an identification of the tasks that would be needed by the participants in order to fulfill the roles envisioned.

TABLE A.2 **Evaluating readiness**

ACTIVITIES/TASK	NUMBER OF HOURS
Basic accounting skills	75
Computer skills and accounting software	20
How to apply for a job	6
Business English and writing skills	15
Psychological support	5
Total hours	**121**

With no existing program to benchmark, the gap analysis was performed based on the previously identified mismatch between workforce skills and market needs.

Stage 3: Design and develop an expanded program

Based on the skills gaps identified, the accounting technician program was designed, comprising 121 hours (table A.2) of training delivered over 22 training days:

The program was designed for immediate impact, with the inclusion of job search skills, as well as psychological support training (including assertiveness training, stress management, etc.). These soft skills would provide an edge to students and help them develop skills that University graduates may not have acquired through their several years of study.

Including Business English and writing skills in the program was also a feature designed to impart immediately usable skills to students. Universities, which operate in an academic environment and are subject government regulations and oversight, may not always have the flexibility to incorporate these studies in their academic programs.

Development of the program materials was undertaken by the trainers, with review and oversight by the collaboration partners. The competency-based nature of the program is visible in its content and design. Technical content included foundational skills such as bookkeeping, managing petty cash, performing bank reconciliations, budgeting, operational analysis, and using Excel.

The Business English and Writing Skills component included the following activities:

- Introducing yourself in English
- Role-playing in an interview setting
- Receiving and making phone calls in English
- Producing a resume in English
- Writing emails in English.

The Psychological Support training included the following topics:

- Explanation of assertiveness and effective communication skills
- Creation of boundaries that can help interpersonal relationships
- Explanation of the stress vulnerability model
- Review of the ABC model of Cognitive Behavioral Therapy
- Monitoring of emotions
- Learning thought errors that elicit biased thoughts that might contribute to distress.

The significant inclusion of soft skills that are particularly relevant in the local context highlights and reflects the importance of these skills in determining a candidate's employability.

Stage 4: Implement the expanded program

The PWAT program was run in three training sites in Palestine. All 72 of the women participating successfully completed the program.

In the course of the delivery of the program, trainers and participant found ways to make the most of resources available to them. Training was applied and interactive, using pair-work, discussions, and practical exercises. The trainers harnessed the diversity of skills and backgrounds of the students by pairing students that were knowledgeable in particular areas with less-knowledgeable students. Some of the students set up a Facebook group to be able to share information, job opportunities, and further professional development opportunities with their colleagues.

Post-survey analysis of the program indicated that the participants believed that the objectives had been met and that they had benefitted from the training and built new skills that would enhance their employability.

NOTE

1. http://www.worldbank.org/en/country/westbankandgaza/publication/palestine-s -economic-outlook--october-2017

REFERENCE

World Bank. 2017. *Report on the Observance of Standards and Codes on Accounting and Auditing: Republic of the Philippines*. World Bank, Washington, DC. © World Bank. https:// openknowledge.worldbank.org/handle/10986/29592.

B

Professional Development and Assessment

APPENDIX B1. USING IAESB'S INTERNATIONAL EDUCATION STANDARDS AS A KEY REFERENCE FOR CBAETC

The International Education Standards™ (IES™) maintained by the International Accounting Education Standards Board™ (IAESB™), as well as the additional guidance provided by IAESB, should be considered a fundamental set of resources for any organization undertaking CBAETC.

The IESs provide guidance on both IPD and CPD, meaning that they serve as valuable tools for developing CBAETC elements for both certification and post-certification.

One of the most important ways that the IESs should be used is with respect to determining the required learning outcomes for the profession. The IESs present requirements for both technical and non-technical learning outcomes of professional accountants.

IES 2 provides, in tabular form, learning outcomes for technical competence across eleven specified competence domains. The learning outcomes are not referred to as competency statements by IAESB, but they bear strong resemblance to the level of granularity found in competency frameworks. Below are extracts from tables B.1–B.3: Learning Outcomes for Technical Competence in paragraph 7 of IES 2 for two competence areas (Financial reporting and accounting and Economics) with the specified level of proficiency to be achieved by the end of IPD. Note that in the IESs, proficiency levels are established at the level of the domain or area, rather than at the learning outcome level.

Some leading PAOs specify proficiency levels for professional accountants at the end of IPD that go beyond those specified by the IESs. For example, at entry point to the profession (i.e., after completing all education, professional training, and assessment programs), SAICA expects the demonstration of an *advanced* level of proficiency for all pervasive qualities and skills and in the competence area Accounting and External Reporting, whereas the IESs require only an *intermediate* proficiency level.

With respect to non-technical competence, IESs 3 and 4 present required learning outcomes in the areas of Professional Skills (IES 3) and Professional Values, Ethics, and Attitudes (IES 4). Again, these learning outcomes inform the

TABLE B.1 **IES 2, Initial Professional Development—technical competence, 2015**

COMPETENCE AREA (LEVEL OF PROFICIENCY)	LEARNING OUTCOMES
(1) Financial accounting and reporting (Intermediate)	(1) Apply accounting principles to transactions and other events. (2) Apply International Financial Reporting Standards (IFRSs) or other relevant standards to transactions and other events. (3) Evaluate the appropriateness of accounting policies used to prepare financial statements. (4) Prepare financial statements, including consolidated financial statements, in accordance with IFRSs. (5) Interpret financial statements and related disclosures. (6) Interpret reports that include non-financial data, for example sustainability reports and integrated reports.
(2) Economics (Foundation)	(1) Describe the fundamental principles of microeconomics and macroeconomics. (2) Describe the effect of changes in macroeconomic indicators on business activity. (c) Explain the different types of market structures, including perfect competition, monopolistic competition, monopoly, and oligopoly.

Source: International Federation of Accountants 2017.

TABLE B.2 **IES 3, Initial Professional Development—professional skills, 2015**

COMPETENCE AREA (LEVEL OF PROFICIENCY)	LEARNING OUTCOMES
(1) Intellectual (Intermediate)	(1) Evaluate information from a variety of sources and perspectives through research, analysis, and integration. (2) Apply professional judgment, including identification and evaluation of alternatives, to reach well-reasoned conclusions based on all relevant facts and circumstances. (3) Identify when it is appropriate to consult with specialists to solve problems and reach conclusions. (4) Apply reasoning, critical analysis, and innovative thinking to solve problems. (5) Recommend solutions to unstructured, multifaceted problems.
(2) Interpersonal and Communication (Intermediate)	(1) Display cooperation and teamwork when working towards organizational goals (2) Communicate clearly and concisely when presenting, discussing and reporting in formal and informal situations, both in writing and orally. (3) …

Source: International Federation of Accountants 2017.

TABLE B.3 **IES 4, Initial Professional Development—professional values, ethics, and attitudes, 2015**

COMPETENCE AREA (LEVEL OF PROFICIENCY)	LEARNING OUTCOMES
(1) Professional skepticism and professional judgment (Intermediate)	(1) Apply a questioning mindset critically to assess financial information and other relevant data. (2) Identify and evaluate reasonable alternatives to reach well-reasoned conclusions based on all relevant facts and circumstances.
(2) Ethical principles (Intermediate)	(1) Explain the nature of ethics. (2) Explain the advantages and disadvantages of rules-based and principles-based approaches to ethics. (3) …

Source: International Federation of Accountants 2017.

competencies required of professional accountants in today's business environment. Excerpts of IESs 3 and 4 are included in tables B.2 and B.3.

Every organization implementing CBAETC should carefully review the IESs, and should also consider the guidance from the IAESB regarding implementing a learning outcomes approach, available at: https://www.ifac.org /publications-resources/guidance-support-implementation-learning -outcomes-approach.

APPENDIX B2. COMPARING SAMPLE COMPETENCY DOMAINS

Competency domains are used to group the technical and enabling competencies into logical groupings that cover the full range of competencies expected of professional accountants. Examples of different approaches are included in table B.4.

IESs 2, 3 and 4 provide a useful starting point to identify competence areas for newly-certified professional accountants (at the end of IPD). They are one

TABLE B.4 **Competency domains: Newly qualified professional accountants**

IAESB IESS	PATHWAYS COMMISSION	CPA CANADA	SAICA
TECHNICAL DOMAINS	**TECHNICAL DOMAINS**	**TECHNICAL DOMAINS**	**TECHNICAL DOMAINS**
• Financial accounting and reporting • Management accounting • Audit and assurance • Finance and financial management • Taxation • Governance, risk management and internal control • Business laws and regulations • Business & organizational environment • Economics • Business strategy and management • Information technology	• Financial accounting & reporting • Operational/management accounting • Auditing and attest services • Governmental accounting & reporting • Other	• Financial reporting • Management accounting • Audit and assurance • Finance • Taxation • Strategy and Governance	• Accounting and external reporting • Management decision-making and control • Auditing and assurance • Financial management • Taxation • Strategy, risk management and governance
Professional values, ethics and attitudes	*Professional integrity, responsibility, and commitment*	*Enabling*	*Pervasive skills*
• Professional skepticism and professional judgment • Ethical principles • Commitment to the public interest	• Behavior/attitude consistent with core values • Ethical knowledge • Ethical reasoning • Professional and legal responsibilities • Commitment to the public interest	• Problem-solving and decision-making • Professional and ethical behavior • Communication • Self-management • Teamwork and leadership	• Ethics and professionalism • Personal attributes • Professional skills
Professional skills	*Professional skills*		
• Intellectual • Interpersonal and communication • Personal • Organizational	• Critical thinking, problem solving • Judgment & decision making • Commitment to learning • Communications/collaboration Leadership • People skills and personality • Managerial skills • Technology skills		

Source: International Federation of Accountants 2017.

of the many sources used by the Pathways Commission as a foundation to develop recommendations for the components of accounting competency.

Perhaps better reflecting the now established utility of IT in the work of a professional accountant, the Pathways Commission recommendations classify IT skills as professional skills, rather than as technical knowledge, and CPA Canada implicitly presumes such skills throughout its technical domains.

IAESB identifies "professional skepticism and professional judgment" as professional values, ethics, and attitudes, whereas the Pathways Commission identifies "critical thinking, problem solving" and "judgment & decision making" as professional skills. CPA Canada simply avoids differentiating between professional skills and professional values, ethics, and attitudes by instead specifying overarching "enabling" competency areas.

It should be noted that these are just different ways of classifying learning outcomes or competencies. Provided that the approach chosen is rational, internally consistent, and practically applied through the program, it really doesn't matter which approach is ultimately used.

APPENDIX B3. SETTING PROFICIENCY LEVELS AT INTERIM POINTS

Proficiency levels are generally specified at the point of certification or licensing, but can also be set at interim points, such as upon entry to a professional program, or on completion of stages within a program.

CPA Canada, for example, specifies minimum proficiency levels at each of the following points in their program:

- On "Entry" to the professional program (representing the expectation of competence for a student graduating university with a degree in business or accounting, and having completed appropriate pre-requisite courses)
- Moving through the CPA professional education program through the "Core" and "Elective" modules; and

TABLE B.5 **Setting proficiency levels**

COMPETENCY STATEMENTS	CORE				ELECTIVES				CAPSTONE		
	ENTRY	C1	C2	CORE	E1 PM	E2 FIN	E3 A5	E4 TAX	CAP 1	CAP 2	
Technical competencies											
4. Audit and assurance											
4.1. Internal control											
4.1.1. Assesses the entity's risk assessment processes	B	A		A			A		>	>	
4.1.2. Evaluates the information system, including the related processes	C	B		B	A		A		>	>	Common Final Evaluation
4.2. Internal and external audit requirements											
4.2.1. Advises on an entry's assurance needs	B			B			A		>	>	
4.2.2. Explains the implications of pending changes in assurance standards	C			C			B		>	>	
4.3. Internal audit projects and external assurance engagements											
4.3.1. Assesses issues related to the undertaking of the engagement of project	B	B		B			A		>	>	

Source: CPA Canada 2018.

Note: "C1" = Core 1 (an integrative module mostly covering financial accounting, audit & assurance, and tax).

"C2" = Core 2 (an integrative module mostly covering internal roles, such as management accounting, strategy & governance, and finance).

"Core" is the combined proficiency level after completing both Core 1 and Core 2.

- At completion of the program following the "Capstone" modules, as well as the "Common Final Evaluation" (a 3-day exam made up primarily of cases).

An excerpt of CPA Canada's Competency Map is included in table B.5. The Electives are:

- E1 (PM) = Performance Management (Strategy, Governance, Management decision-making)
- E2 (FIN) = Finance
- E3 (AS) = Assurance
- E4 (TAX) = Taxation.

"Cap 1" and "Cap 2" are the two Capstone courses that focus on integrating competencies, rather than specifically developing new or additional competence or proficiency.

For the different competency statements, the required proficiency level changes depending on the elective chosen. Electives add more depth, and the proficiency level of the most closely related competencies will be higher.

The ">" symbol under Capstones 1 and 2 indicates that the proficiency level from the prior program module completed is continued. For example, if a student only completed Core 1, then they are expected to achieve proficiency level "B" on competency 4.1.2, whereas level "A" is expected of students who also completed either elective E1 or E3. These expected levels carry through to the Common Final Evaluation.

Note also that candidates who are planning on becoming licensed to practice public accounting are expected to complete both the Assurance and Taxation electives, thereby requiring higher proficiency levels for some competency areas particularly associated with that role.

REFERENCES

CPA (Chartered Professional Accountants) Canada. 2018. *The Chartered Professional Accountant Competency Map: Understanding the Competencies a Candidate Must Demonstrate to Become a CPA*. Issued and revised in December 2018. https://www.cpacanada.ca/en/become-a-cpa/pathways-to-becoming-a-cpa/national-education-resources/the-cpa-competency-map.

International Federation of Accountants. 2017. *Handbook of International Education Pronouncements*. New York: IFAC.

Examples

APPENDIX C1. FRAMEWORK/PRINCIPLE-BASED TEACHING EXTRACT FROM THE UNIVERSITY OF CAPE TOWN COLLEGE OF ACCOUNTING FACULTY HANDBOOK

Reprinted with permission from The University of Cape Town College of Accounting, Cape Town, South Africa. Any changes to the original material are the sole responsibility of the authors (and/or publisher) and have not been reviewed or endorsed by The University of Cape Town College of Accounting.

2.3 A case for framework/principle-based teaching

This section of the handbook is intended to indicate why framework or principle-based teaching is appropriate in an accounting education environment and to provide some practical guidance for doing and assessing framework-based teaching.

2.3.1 What is framework/principle-based teaching and why is it appropriate

The syllabus that accounting students need to understand is large, some of it complex and much of what is included is likely to be out of date in a few years. In addition, the context in which businesses operate changes fast, which implies that accounting graduates will need to deal with new types of transactions, industries with which they are not familiar, as well as the changing information needs of diverse groups of users. The approach that is followed in educating our students must take those factors into consideration. This means that we must ensure that our students have the ability to understand the material covered, cope with the perceived volume of the syllabus, and develop the ability to apply principles in unfamiliar scenarios, as well as the ability to cope with new developments once they have graduated.

The combined approach that we take in preparing and presenting lecture material, the tutorials that are used to support the lectures, and the way in which we assess will all strongly influence the benefit that students will derive from a course. A good course and lecturer should be judged on the long-term benefits a student develops and not on the popularity of the lecturer in course evaluations or the marks that students receive. Students with a firm grasp of the key principles will be able to retain their knowledge, build on their knowledge as they progress to more senior courses and apply those principles to unfamiliar situations that they should encounter in exams and will encounter in their professional lives. An educational approach focusing on the key principles and frameworks will achieve that, whereas an educational approach focusing on the mechanics and exceptions will not.

Framework or principle-based teaching emphasizes the key principles underpinning the topic being lectured. This enables students to identify what calculations and techniques are similar, why they are similar, and also to understand the need for any differences that may arise. Where students are able to discern that the principles applied in different aspects of the syllabus are the same, as well as understand the need for any variations on the general principles, this will have the impact of reducing the syllabus, constantly reinforcing the principles and giving the students the tools to deal with new scenarios where the principles should be applied and what variations may be appropriate.

As lecturers, one aspect of our role is to help students develop the ability to identify the appropriate principles to apply in developing a solution to a problem in real life (or more urgently, an exam question as a university student), as well as understanding how to apply the principles. It is equally important to be able to identify and justify which approach or techniques are inappropriate to use in dealing with a transaction or issue. An educational approach that focuses on the thought process of why a technique is used as opposed to the mechanics of how to apply a technique will develop a stronger understanding of the particular topic and the subject as a whole.

Teaching students the mechanics of how to deal with an aspect of the syllabus without making it clear what principles are being applied and why those principles are appropriate will only give students the skills to deal with examples that are similar to those that they have seen before. As students need to be able to continue learning, deal with unfamiliar scenarios and questions that integrate different issues and examine the same topic using different approaches, this is clearly both inappropriate and inadequate.

In some respects, the principles are clearly articulated in a document, and in others they are less accessible but no less important. For example, the Conceptual Framework for Financial Reporting sets out the concepts that underlie the preparation and presentation of financial statements. Those concepts are the basic principles that underpin the more detailed explanations of the principles in topic specific financial reporting standards.

2.3.2 A good lecture versus a bad lecture

A good lecture will result in a student understanding what the basic principles are that need to be applied in dealing with that topic, and how that topic fits into the subject matter as a whole. A bad lecture will result in the students having pockets of information that is not linked to the subject as a whole with a knowledge of the exceptions and complexities but not the basic concepts. A good lecture is also one that a student leaves understanding the key principles and how that topic fits into the big picture of the subject as a whole. It should start by indicating the relevance of the topic to the professional environment, for example, how it will influence decisions, impact on the risks or cash flows of the organization. Students who understand the relevance of the topic that is being covered are more likely to make an effort to get on top of the material.

The explanations for the appropriate treatment should start with the basic concepts and develop from there to the more specific criteria for that topic. For example, in financial reporting a lecture on employee benefits could start with a true-life case study of unrecorded liabilities from a post-retirement medical scheme, move onto the definition of a liability and then focus on why employee benefit reporting may require a treatment that applies the definition and recognition criteria on a different basis from that which applies to other liabilities.

A course evaluation that indicates that the lecturer spends too much time on the basics and not enough time on the more complex aspects is usually an indicator of a good lecturer. Our role is to make sure that the average student has a firm grasp of the key issues—the brighter student will work out the complexities for themselves if necessary.

A good lecture should have short examples to illustrate the key principles where that is necessary. A class example is likely to be different from the tutorial and test questions that students are expected to know as it should be focused only on the principle which it is intended to demonstrate. Generally, the simpler the example is, the more effective it is likely to be. A bad lecture example would focus on the mechanics of the calculations as opposed to the principles that are underpinning those calculations.

2.3.3 The relationship between lectures, workshops and tutorials and tests

The purpose of a lecture should be to ensure that the students understand the basic principles that they will be expected to apply. A student should not expect to be lectured on every application of the principle that they are likely to encounter. One application of an approach may be used in lectures, with other approaches demonstrated at workshops or tutorials, that is, in an environment in which students would be expected to work out for themselves how to apply a particular principle. For example, a discussion on depreciation in a junior financial reporting course should focus on the need to write down an asset as it is consumed (i.e., no future economic benefits) and could do the calculations on the straight-line basis. A tutorial question could explain the concept of reducing balance depreciation and when it would be more appropriate and leave the students to work out how to do the calculations and process the amounts on their own.

If a lecture is going to be principle-based and use simple illustrative examples to demonstrate those principles, there is going to be a significant difference in the standard of the lecture examples and the assessment questions. That gap needs to be bridged by carefully selecting tutorials that are designed to bridge that gap in manageable stages. At least one, and probably more, of the tutorials must be of the standard that a student would be expected to apply in an exam scenario.

Principle-based teaching does not imply that students should not be exposed to more complicated applications of those principles. What it does imply is that the principles should be emphasized in lectures and that the students should test their understanding of those principles by being given examples that enable them to apply those principles in combination with other related issues or in more complex transactions. For example, a lecture may deal with the principles behind the calculation and implication of an effective rate calculation using a settlement date that is coterminous with the reporting date. A student who understands the principle should be able to apply those principles where the year-end differs from the settlement date, or where the instrument is a foreign currency instrument. Lecturing all the possible scenarios that they may encounter will not help the students identify weaknesses in their understanding or their ability to apply principles to different circumstances.

When selecting tutorials for a principle-based teaching, the basic philosophy of ensuring that the students understand and are able to apply the basic principles should be the main consideration. This implies that the tutorials should be carefully selected to ensure that the students are given appropriate questions to test whether they understand the principles and whether they would be able to apply those principles in an unfamiliar scenario. Generally, fewer tutorials with more discussion on "what if..." is more effective than many tutorials. Students should not expect to have a tutorial on every aspect that could be examined, as that will send the message that they are only expected to be able to handle applications that they have seen before. More reflection on fewer tutorials will generate more understanding than superficial attempts at many tutorials. We need to resist the temptation to provide too many tutorials, revision packs, workshops etc.

Immature and short-sighted students would like their lecturers to coach them on how to answer a particular type of question by giving them a prescribed manner in which to do their workings, and then to make sure that that approach is used to answer all the tutorials and the exam question. While the students may like that approach and it does make marking much easier, it will result in students who are only able to answer questions on that topic if they are set in a certain manner and only so long as they are able to recall the approach (formula, layout, etc.) that they have been taught. This is completely contrary to the concept of principle and framework-based teaching and will result in students who struggle to retain, integrate and build on their knowledge.

2.3.4 Techniques for ensuring that students are focusing on principles

There are a number of different techniques that can be used by lecturers to ensure that students understand what the key principles are and how they should be applied, and those tasked with assessing the quality of a course can use to ensure that the academic approach is principle and not rule/detail driven.

1. **Objective tests:** (see separate note) Every module presented should have teaching objectives, that is, what principles is that module intended to introduce or reinforce. On a regular basis (e.g., weekly tutorial) a short test question that is intended to identify if the key principle has been understood is useful feedback for the student and the lecturer

2. **Discussion questions:** The inclusion of discussion questions in tests is often a better indicator of the extent to which a student has understood the principles than a question requiring calculations. A question that asks the student to justify an approach suggested or indicate why it is inappropriate is often a useful indicator of how well a student understands the principles

3. **Unfamiliar scenarios and applications:** Presenting students with a question that tests principles that they should understand in a scenario that they would not have seen before tests their ability to comprehend the scenario, identify the appropriate principle and apply those principles. An example could be a discussion question on the appropriate accounting for rain water in a farmer's dam which is a test of their ability to apply the asset definition

4. **Unpredictability of tutorial and test questions:** Students should expect to get test questions that do not follow the same approach as their lecture and

tutorial examples. This clearly implies that their tutorial questions should be diverse in order to appropriately prepare them for that type of testing and to reinforce that they need to understand the principles as they will not be able to reproduce answers that they have seen before. This can be done by changing the testing style, for example, a discussion question on a topic that is usually a calculation or by combining different topics into one question

5. **Identify key principles in tutorial/workshop examples:** When a student has completed a question, they should be able to identify the key principles that that question addressed. Asking students to make a note of the key principles in a question is a good indicator of whether they can identify what the key principles are as well as reinforcing their understanding of those principles

6. **Mark plans in solutions to clearly identify principles for which they are awarded:** A mark plan that indicates the principle that the mark is allocated to instead of the amount for which it is allocated will both demonstrate that the marker carries through errors in doing the marking as well as reinforcing the principles that should have been applied

7. **Review students' scripts from a test:** A variety of different approaches taken by students when answering a question will indicate that the students were taught using a principle driven approach. Where all the students are using a similar approach in answering a question, that is an indication that they have been taught how to do their workings and probably also exposed to worked examples illustrating that approach. Those students have been coached to answer that question and are unlikely to be able to apply those principles in different scenarios

8. **Providing unstructured and irrelevant information in a question:** Students that clearly understand the principles should know what information is relevant in answering the question. They should therefore be able to gather the relevant information from different parts of the question and also know which information has no bearing on the solution.

2.3.5 Practical examples of framework-based teaching

Deferred tax
A student entering Financial Reporting III (FR3) should be able to understand the difference between an event/transaction/business case and the accounting thereof. While a transaction could be complicated, it should be understood that the accounting thereof (certainly at a FR2 and even at a FR3 level) is fairly straight forward, in that there is a debit and a credit entry. To be able to prepare the journal entry, students must be able to:

• Identify the reporting entity
• Identify and measure the assets/liabilities of that entity (applying definitions, recognition criteria, etc.)
• Identify equity as the residual and understand that the changes in equity could be recognized directly in equity, P/L, OCI and as prior year restatements.

Deferred tax should be introduced prior to groups. The issues should not be dealt with at a complex level but as an introduction to the concepts and bedding down those fundamentals. It is important to recognize that once students have dealt with groups, and the students are not asking why there is no deferred tax at a groups level then it means that they have either (largely) missed the point in groups, in deferred tax or both. With respect to deferred tax, the most important point is that the issue is not deferred tax. The issue is accounting for income taxes, of which deferred tax is one component, the other being current tax. As the accounting of a transaction is being reflected in its entirety, that is, including the tax effects and because current tax is based on a different set of rules, deferred tax could be recognized. This is probably easiest explained in a group scenario where every entity is a separate taxable entity (for reporting for tax purposes) but for accounting purposes the group as the reporting entity is seen as one economic entity. The point is whether you are looking at current tax/deferred tax:

- You still need to be able to identify a reporting entity
- Identify an asset/liability that has tax consequences, which themselves give rise to assets and liabilities
- Recognize changes in those assets or liabilities somewhere ... .

APPENDIX C2. PAO OUTSOURCING THROUGH PARTNERING WITH TERTIARY INSTITUTIONS—SAICA EXAMPLE

Collaboration between PAOs and tertiary institutions is an important method of ensuring the efficient use of resources. Universities and other tertiary institutions are often well-equipped to develop competence in students who wish to become professional accountants. For these partnerships to be effective, however, it is essential that the PAO provide clear guidelines as to the requirements that must be met to become an accredited provider of IPD.

The South African Institute of Chartered Accountants (SAICA) outsources all the necessary professional accountancy education to accredited universities. SAICA retains responsibility for the qualifying examinations that, together with relevant practical experience, permit certification and access to the profession. The basic path to membership in the SAICA is as follows (some steps are completed in parallel):

- Complete the Certificate of Theory in Accounting (CTA), an academic program that requires 4 years formal accounting education at a SAICA accredited university
- Start a formal training program with an SAICA accredited Training Office.
- Pass the Initial Test of Competence (ITC)
- Complete a minimum of 20 months of a registered training contract with a SAICA accredited Training Office
- Complete a professional program with a SAICA accredited provider
- Pass the Assessment of Professional Competence (APC) evaluation
- Complete the SAICA Training Program (STC), requiring a mandatory period of practical experience (3–5 years including the previously-noted 20 months) in a SAICA accredited Training Office, under the supervision of an experienced Chartered Accountant.

SAICA's mapping—and associated detailed guidance for external parties it accredits to provide formal learning and practical experience—provides a good practice example of the resources and program elements that support successful PAO-university partnerships. The guidance is posted on SAICA's website:

- SAICA's Detailed Guidance for the Academic Programmed: Competencies of a CA(SA) at the point of the ITC (assessment of core technical knowledge) (2014)[1]
- SAICA's Detailed Guidance for the Professional Programmed: Competencies of a CA(SA) at the point of the Assessment of Professional Competence (2015)[2]
- SAICA's Training Programmed: Implementation Guide (January 2016)[3].

SAICA's Competency Framework details competencies required of Chartered Accountants at entry point to the profession (i.e., at the end of IPD: after completion of the academic program, the training program, the professional program, and all associated assessments). SAICA specifies proficiency levels for each learning outcome at three consecutive assessment points that an aspiring professional accountant must pass to successfully reach the end of IPD, namely on completion of the ITC, APC, and STP.

The example below shows SAICA's 2015 mapping for the competency area Accounting and External Reporting at ITC, APC, and STP. This table C.1 details the proficiency level required for each competency and provides universities

TABLE C.1 **SAICA's 2015 mapping for the competency area Accounting and External Reporting at ITC, APC, and STP**

ACCOUNTING AND EXTERNAL REPORTING[a] LEARNING OUTCOMES	ITC	APC	STP
1. Analyzes financial reporting needs and establishes the necessary systems			
(a) Identifies the appropriate reporting framework	Advanced[b]	Advanced	Advanced[c]
(b) Analyzes financial reporting needs	Advanced	Advanced	Advanced
(c) Develops or evaluates reporting processes to support financial reporting	Advanced	Advanced	Advanced
(d) Develops reliable information	Advanced	Advanced	Advanced
(e) Establishes or enhances financial reporting using IT	Intermediate[d]	Intermediate	Advanced
2. Conducts external financial reporting			
(a) Develops or evaluates accounting policies in accordance with IFRS	Advanced	Advanced	Advanced
(b) Accounts for the entity's routine transactions	Advanced	Advanced	Advanced
(c) Accounts for the entity's non-routine transactions	Advanced	Advanced	Advanced
(d) Prepares financial statements using IFRS	Advanced	Advanced	Advanced
(e) Prepares or evaluates financial statement note disclosure	Advanced	Advanced	Advanced
(f) Explains the financial statement results and balances to stakeholders	Advanced	Advanced	Advanced
(g) Maintains awareness of key ideas and principles of proposed financial reporting standards changes	Foundation[e]	Foundation	Advanced
(h) Considers the integrity of the financial information in the integrated report	Foundation	Foundation	Advanced
3. Conducts specialized reporting			
(a) Identifies and analyzes specific reporting obligations	Intermediate	Intermediate	Advanced
(b) Identifies regulatory and other filing requirements	Foundation	Foundation	Advanced
(c) Identifies and analyzes non-financial reporting needs	Intermediate	Intermediate	Advanced
(d) Conducts external and internal non-financial reporting	Intermediate	Intermediate	Advanced

Source: South African Institute of Chartered Accountants (SAICA), https://www.saico.co.za.

a. Learning outcomes and proficiency levels for the competence area Accounting and External Reporting SAICA extracted from SAICA's Detailed Guidance for the Professional Program: Competencies of a CA(SA) at the point of the Assessment of Professional Competence (2015): p. 14 (see https://www.saica .co.za/Portals/0/LearnersStudents/documents/Detailed_Guidance_to_the_Competency_Framework_APC_2015.pdf).

b. For ease of understanding in this guide we describe SAICA's Level X as Advanced. SAICA describes its Level X as follows: "Completes all elements of a specified task successfully and an advanced understanding of the subject matter is consequently required. Relevant pervasive skills and reflective capacity should be demonstrated at an advanced level. Technical skills expected to be demonstrated at this level include, for example, performing complex calculations and concluding on an appropriate course of action. Proficiency at level X is demonstrated when the problem is clearly identified and thoroughly analyzed, or when a situation is evaluated and useful recommendations are made. This level of proficiency includes level A and I proficiencies."

c. For ease of understanding in this guide we describe SAICA's Level C as Advanced. SAICA describes its Level C as follows: "COMPULSORY (to advanced level)." In this context Advanced is "Comprehensive understanding of the concepts and techniques and must be able to apply these concepts and techniques in complex situations or environments."

d. For ease of understanding in this guide we describe SAICA's Level I as Intermediate. SAICA describes its Level I as follows: "Demonstrates an understanding of the requirements of the task and identifies and applies the required professional skills, including basic quantitative and qualitative analysis, to perform the task on a preliminary basis (recognizing that a review by more senior staff is still necessary). An intermediate understanding of the subject matter is required. Complex calculations are not required. Integration with other competencies is straightforward and is of limited complexity. Level I includes level A proficiency."

e. For ease of understanding in this guide we describe SAICA's Level A as Foundation. SAICA describes its Level A as follows: "Requires an awareness of the key ideas and principles within the area. Demonstration of technical expertise or detailed knowledge in this area is not required. The candidate identifies and explains the significance of the competency, and the types of circumstances in which it would arise or be applied."

and other partners with the clarity needed to plan their own programs that they wish to have accredited by SAICA.

APPENDIX C3. CONTINUOUS REVIEW—AICPA EXAMPLE

The American Institute of Certified Public Accountants (AICPA) provides a good practice example of the process of continuous review. Its process for a single review can take a number of years. For example, the design changes to the AICPA's Uniform CPA Examination effective from April 2017 are the result of a comprehensive project launched in 2014. That project involved[4]:

- Research and analysis: Identifying the knowledge and skills required of newly licensed CPAs by gathering information from stakeholders using a variety of methods, including focus groups, interviews, an Invitation to Comment, and a comprehensive nationwide survey and input from the AICPA Board of Examiners (BOE) and its Practice Analysis Sponsor Group, the BOE Sponsor Advisory Group, Content Committee, and its content subcommittees
- Public consultation: Exposure Draft *Maintaining the Relevance of the Uniform CPA Examination* issued for public comment, representing the culmination of in-depth research, critical analysis of data, best practices in test development, and the collective thinking of leaders in the profession
- Finalization: In February 2016, following a thorough review of all comments, the BOE unanimously approved the final content, structure, and design of the Exam
- Launch: The "new" Exam launched in April 2017.

Perhaps most importantly, the process revealed that the profession believes it is critically important that newly licensed CPAs are competent in recognizing issues, identifying errors, challenging assumptions, and applying both professional judgment and skepticism. Consequently, from April 2017, the AICPA's Uniform CPA Examination will have an increased emphasis on testing higher-order cognitive skills (that include, but are not limited to, critical thinking, problem-solving, and analytical ability) by including additional task-based simulations (TBSs) on the Exam and increasing the background material and data in a TBS that will require candidates to determine what information is or is not relevant to the question. The AICPA assesses this as being more reflective of the nature of challenges newly licensed CPAs encounter in practice.

The AICPA explicitly acknowledges that changes in the profession and to technology necessitates annual assessment of the content and skills tested in its Uniform CPA Examination, which could lead to extending the assessment of evaluation tasks in the future.

Moreover, with a view to further testing professional judgment/skepticism and writing assessment, the AICPA has accelerated research into more advanced, automated essay-scoring technology and, with the assistance of third-party testing experts, is continuing to research potential alternatives to evaluating professional skepticism, which could result in the development of new types of questions for the Exam.

NOTES

1. https://www.saica.co.za/Portals/0/LearnersStudents/documents/Detailed_Guidance_to
_the_competency_framework_for_the_academic_programme_Updated_and_approved
_July_2014.pdf
2. https://www.saica.co.za/Portals/0/LearnersStudents/documents/Detailed_Guidance_to
_the_Competency_Framework_APC_2015.pdf
3. https://www.saica.co.za/trainees/training/theca2010trainingprogramme/tabid/1657
/language/en-US/default.aspx
4. See http://www.aicpa.org/BecomeACPA/CPAExam/nextexam/DownloadableDocuments
/2016-practice-analysis-final-report.pdf